Jewcy

SUNY SERIES IN CONTEMPORARY JEWISH LITERATURE AND CULTURE

EZRA CAPPELL, EDITOR

Dan Shiffman, *College Bound:*
The Pursuit of Education in Jewish American Literature, 1896–1944

Eric J. Sundquist, editor, *Writing in Witness:*
A Holocaust Reader

Noam Pines, *The Infrahuman: Animality in Modern Jewish Literature*

Oded Nir, *Signatures of Struggle:*
The Figuration of Collectivity in Israeli Fiction

Zohar Weiman-Kelman, *Queer Expectations:*
A Genealogy of Jewish Women's Poetry

Richard J. Fein, translator, *The Full Pomegranate:*
Poems of Avrom Sutzkever

Victoria Aarons and Holli Levitsky, editors,
New Directions in Jewish American and
Holocaust Literatures: Reading and Teaching

Jennifer Cazenave, *An Archive of the Catastrophe:*
The Unused Footage of Claude Lanzmann's Shoah

Ruthie Abeliovich, *Possessed Voices:*
Aural Remains from Modernist Hebrew Theater

Victoria Nesfield and Philip Smith, editors,
The Struggle for Understanding: Elie Wiesel's Literary Works

Ezra Cappell and Jessica Lang, editors,
Off the Derech: Leaving Orthodox Judaism

Nancy E. Berg and Naomi B. Sokoloff, editors,
Since 1948: Israeli Literature in the Making

Patrick Chura, *Michael Gold: The People's Writer*

Nahma Sandrow, *Yiddish Plays for Reading and Performance*

Alisha Kaplan and Tobi Aaron Kahn, *Qorbanot*

Sara R. Horowitz, Amira Bojadzija-Dan, and Julia Creet, editors
Shadows in the City of Light: Images of Paris in
Postwar French Jewish Writing

Alana Szobel, *Flesh of My Flesh: Sexual Violence in Modern Hebrew Literature*

Ranen Omer Sherman, *Amos Oz: The Legacy of a Writer*
in Israel and Beyond

Adi Mahalel, *The Radical Isaac: I. L. Peretz and the Rise of Jewish Socialism*

Jewcy

Jewish Queer Lesbian Feminisms
for the Twenty-First Century

Edited by

MARLA BRETTSCHNEIDER

SUNY
PRESS

Cover design by Sharon Gershoni and Aimee Harrison

Published by State University of New York Press, Albany

For information, contact State University of New York Press, Albany, NY
www.sunypress.edu

Library of Congress Cataloging-in-Publication Data

Name: Brettschneider, Marla, editor.
Title: Jewcy : Jewish queer lesbian feminisms for the twenty-first century /
    edited by Marla Brettschneider.
Description: Albany : State University of New York Press, [2024] | Series:
    SUNY series in contemporary Jewish literature and culture | Includes
    bibliographical references and index.
Identifiers: LCCN 2023019232 | ISBN 9781438496276 (hardcover : alk. paper) |
    ISBN 9781438496283 (ebook) | ISBN 9781438496269 (pbk. : alk. paper)
Subjects: LCSH: Jewish lesbians—History—21st century. | Jewish women—Sexual
    Behavior—21st century. | Jewish lesbians—Identity—History—21st century. |
    Queer theory—History—21st century.
Classification: LCC BM729.H65 J49 2024 | DDC 306.76/63089924—dc23/eng/20231002
LC record available at https://lccn.loc.gov/2023019232

10 9 8 7 6 5 4 3 2 1

This book is dedicated to:

Evelyn Torton Beck
Irina Klepfisz
Carolivia Herron
Sharon Cohen
Joan Nestle

Contents

Acknowledgments

Jewcy, this book, is luscious. Luscious, subversive, thought-provoking, as are our lives, communities, and creations. *Jewcy* takes its name from a Jewish activist cohort organized some decades ago. They created much for each other and for us all in their ongoing work together. See below for some background. Gratitude to the activists and to Arthur Waskow.

Many thanks to Esther Rothblum for engaging me to edit the special Jewish issue of the *Journal of Lesbian Studies*. That project was later released as a book by Routledge with the title *Jewish Lesbian Scholarship in a Time of Change*. The work on *Jewcy* developed out of work on these earlier initiatives, in which I grew to appreciate in new ways the trajectory of excluding lesbians, women, and at times feminists in much of our fantastic queer Jewish activism and scholarship.

I thank Nina Judith Katz for her editing and also Jason Guberman of the American Sephardi Federation for his generous brainstorming and sharing the wealth of his and the ASF's resources and contacts.

Many folks have been involved in the creation of this work, some of whom may realize that and some of whom likely do not. In addition to those to whom this work is dedicated, among those who need to be recognized by name are Ruthie Berman, Connie Kurtz, Martha Ackelsberg, Judith Plaskow, Carol Conaway, Melanie Kaye/Kantrowitz (z"l), Sabrina Sojourner, Rebecca Alpert, Abby Wells, Julie Enszer, Savina Teubal (z"l), Elana Dykwomon (z"l), Judith Katz, Chani Getter, Max Strassfeld, Penina Weinberg, Federica Francesconi, and Rebecca Winer.

Many thanks to the University of New Hampshire Department of Women's and Gender Studies, Department of Political Science, and College of Liberal Arts and their hardworking and supportive staff. This includes many student research assistants over the years, including Ben

McKillop, Marina Cardoso-Vianna-Vaz, Patrick Baga, Caroline Hall, Bethany Kaminsky, Alden Reed, and Toby Afolayan. Much gratitude to the Hadassah-Brandeis Institute, Lisa Fishbayne-Joffe, and the staff and student researchers, including Sofia Siegel, Leah Trachtenberg, and Joelle Galatan.

James Peltz and those at SUNY Press have been supportive for many years, keeping this volume on track through the difficult COVID-19 years. Thank you to the anonymous external reviewers and all those at SUNY who have helped this book come to be.

There have been Lyft drivers who loaned me their phone-charger cords for work that spilled into a ride, who graciously let me speak too loudly into their right ear during an editing meeting, and who wished me well with my "Jewish project"; tech support whizzes who helped out and offered their analysis, "Jewish and lesbian, that's got to be hard"; and so many more.

B'not Esh has continued to sustain me over these three decades. The Feminism, Zionism, and Antisemitism group has also long been a lifeline.

Good colleagues, friends, and family make it all possible. Thanks to Dianne Esses and Sarra Lev, Jane Litman and Sonja Pilz, Lanie Resnick, Alexandra Adler, Ana Gomes, and Dawn Rose for support getting me through. Endless appreciations to Nina and Beth, Toni and Paris.

Regarding the "Jewcy" that inspired the title of this volume, Arthur Waskow writes for this occasion:

> The name, the pun "Jewcy," came with laughter and learning from a group of young Jews who had spent a week of learning and laughter. They had been called together by the Shalom Center to learn to unite social action with spiritual practice. For example, there is an ancient Jewish day, Tisha B'Av, of fasting and mourning in sorrow for the destruction of two holy temples in Jerusalem by the Babylonian and Roman Empires. They asked: Could we draw on this grief for the past and turn it toward transformation of the future—by lifting that day of mourning the destruction of our sacred Temple Earth in the climate crisis brought on by modern Corporate Carbon Empires? Every reinterpretation is a pun. Every pun brings laughter to heal a world of tears.

Introduction

Jewcy: Jewish Queer Lesbian Feminisms for the Twenty-First Century

MARLA BRETTSCHNEIDER

In a tribute to, and enacting of, the diasporic, this volume presents the rich diversity of US Jewish life from a perspective centering lesbian and queer Jewish feminist issues. *Jewcy* addresses readers from an array of communities and should be particularly interesting for those who know little about this subject. In the 1970s, the field of Jewish lesbian studies launched a few exciting decades of extensive publishing, after which it basically went silent in the early 2000s. Too few works in queer studies have focused on Jewish women, feminists, or lesbians. *Jewcy* seeks to redirect an otherwise welcome fecundity in queer studies that has problematically left a dearth of new works explicitly by or about lesbians and/ or women of various gender identities, as well as of works centering Jews and Jewish matters of import. Additionally, despite efforts in both Jewish and queer studies, whiteness and Ashkenazi voices continue to define these fields. This work presents a vibrant diversity of authors speaking to a fresh slate of Jewish feminist lesbian queer issues.

In the past few years, we have seen a resurgence of interest in published works in the area. Correcting a twenty-first-century shift away from explicitly feminist and lesbian investigations in Jewish queer studies and in LBGTQ+ studies, *Jewcy* signals a new trend of original works in the field that is explicitly lesbian, queer, Jewish, and feminist. The founding period of out Jewish lesbian collective action and publishing emerged at a time of various lacunae. In the 1970s, the field of Jewish studies was not yet publishing many women, let alone presenting feminist, lesbian, and/or queer work. Feminist studies was nearly devoid of work on Jewish subjects as well as of lesbian writings. The then-new field of lesbian studies did not reflect Jewish activity. As queer activism and publishing began to develop, Jewish women and lesbian issues were largely left out. In addition, all these fields lacked diversity in terms of communities and modes of critical analysis such as race, ethnicity, religion, and class. Any underrepresentation of BIPOC in these fields also will generally mean that there is a dearth of Jews, as Jews are present in each of these communities.

The recent revival that *Jewcy* highlights does not merely begin where the earlier vibrant period stopped. The new works inherit the significant legacy of the founding period of dynamic Jewish lesbian activism and writing as well as the ensuing decades of Jewish queering. For example, *Jewcy* innovates in not bifurcating the categories of lesbian and queer, as more activists and thinkers are now claiming self-definition in ways that were difficult or deemed unacceptable in our communities for some time, as well as in exciting new ways. Additionally, *Jewcy* embraces diversity in numerous vectors, not merely adding "other" elements to the existent conceptualizations and imagined horizons of what are and can be Jewish and lesbian and queer feminisms; we ground ourselves in diversity as we explore our Jewish lesbian queer feminist lives and worlds. What might a Jewish, lesbian, queer, feminist world be like without essentialist foundations—as Hannah Arendt called it, without banisters? In *Jewcy*, we hope to continue such experimentation, deepening and broadening not only our field but all its mutually constitutive fields of Jewish, queer, feminist, critical race and ethnicity, decolonial, and class-based studies and all of their corresponding communities. How might this expand our experiences, possibilities, and activism?

Those interested in a brief overview of work of Jewish lesbian relevance from earlier periods ranging from antiquity to modernity may find the entry "Lesbianism" in *The Shalvi/Hyman Encyclopedia of Jewish Women* helpful.[1] Rebecca Alpert and I contributed to this succinct yet wide-ranging entry that covers not only modernity but also, given Alpert's expertise, biblical times (1000–165 BCE), rabbinic times (165 BCE–900 CE), and the Middle Ages (900–1700). In our discussion of the late modern era (1800–1945), we introduce Sholem Asch's Yiddish *Got fun Nekome*

(God of vengeance), which was the first play with a lesbian theme to be performed on the US stage; Gertrude Stein and Alice B. Toklas; anarchist activist Pauline Newman; and social reformer Lillian Wald.

Starting in the 1970s, the new field of Jewish lesbian studies burst onto the English-language scene and enabled a plethora of Jewish queer volumes. These works followed closely on the burgeoning fields of feminist, lesbian, gay, bi, trans, intersex, and queer studies, and they joined emerging challenges to the white Christo-normativity of these fields.

Adrienne Rich published actively as a lesbian starting in the mid-1970s; Judith Plaskow and her coeditor, Carol Christ, released their key feminist spirituality reader, *Womanspirit Rising*, in 1979;[2] and in 1982 Evelyn Torton Beck's pivotal *Nice Jewish Girls: A Lesbian Anthology* came out. Savina Teubal published the path-clearing *Sarah the Priestess* in 1984, and Irena Klepfisz and Melanie Kaye/Kantrowitz released their ground-breaking *The Tribe of Dina* in 1986. In 1989, Plaskow and Christ put out their follow-up, *Weaving the Visions*. In this period, Jewish lesbian groups and communities were quickly multiplying and flourishing in religious movements, the arts, politics, and writings of all genres.[3] By the 2000s, however, Jewish lesbian publishing mostly fell silent, although we find a welcome exception in some outstanding works in Jewish trans studies.

Even during the period of greatest activity, Jewish lesbians continued to face exclusion in organizational and academic life as Jews, feminists, women, lesbians, and/or BIPOC, and this exclusion has continued. Jewish lesbian work is still rarely published in lesbian and feminist academic journals outside of Jewish studies, and lesbian-focused articles tend not to appear in the top ten Jewish studies journals. Additionally, as Jewish lesbians have sought to overcome exclusions over time, these efforts have themselves produced new forms of exclusion. Speaking in the name of Jewish lesbians and dykes often excludes or marginalizes bisexuals, trans lesbians, and others. Although some volumes feature non-Ashkenazi and non-white Jewish lesbian feminists, racial, ethnic, and other forms of diversity remain largely lacking in most Jewish lesbian feminist writing, as does scholarly work on Jewish lesbian queer diversity.

In the last few years, the field of Jewish lesbian studies has begun to reemerge with the publication of a few important volumes. A special issue of the *Journal of Lesbian Studies* (*JoLS*) called *Jewish Lesbians: New Work in the Field*, a project initiated by Esther Rothblum, was the first effort in this revaluing of Jewish lesbian work.[4] Published in January 2019 and edited by me, this was the first volume in Jewish lesbian studies in about a decade. It is academic in style and was then adapted and later published as a book, *Jewish Lesbian Scholarship in a Time of Change*, in 2023.[5]

Soon after work on the *JoLS* issue was completed, I began working on this volume. At that time, Joy Ladin published her 2018 *The Soul of the Stranger: Reading God and Torah from a Transgender Perspective*.[6] In this project, the poet and scholar reads well-known Torah stories—that assume human beings are neither male nor female—through her transgender experience and critical perspective. She demonstrates how these stories and new readings speak to practical transgender challenges today and to new understandings of the Torah's portrayals of God. After some years of creative work, veteran Jewish lesbian writers Elana Dykewomon and Judith Katz produced *To Be a Jewish Dyke in the 21st Century*, a special issue of *Sinister Wisdom: A Multicultural Lesbian Literary & Art Journal*, in 2021.[7] This work responds to the critical loss of Jewish lesbian voices and provides an ode and update to *Sinister Wisdom*'s landmark *The Tribe of Dina*, edited by Kaye/Kantrowitz and Klepfisz thirty-five years prior. More wide-ranging in style than the *JoLS* issue, this work is an important contribution. Of further interest in these new paths in queer lesbian feminist work, including trans and intersex studies, in 2022 Jane Rachel Litman and Jakob Hero-Shaw published *Liberating Gender for Jews and Allies: The Wisdom of Transkeit*.[8] Feminist and diverse, the edited work centers trans Jewish life in short chapters that make a valuable contribution. Also in 2022, Max Strassfeld published his *Trans Talmud: Androgynes and Eunuchs in Rabbinic Literature*.[9] His work centers texts in rabbinic literature that also support the project of transgender history; in *Trans Talmud*, Strassfeld's work beyond a gender binary in these ancient Jewish texts helps us to transform law and the boundaries of our communities today, significant for queers, lesbians, transfolk, feminists, Jews, and us all. Most recently, in 2023, Sarra Lev published her book-length work *And the Sages Did Not Know: Early Rabbinic Approaches to Intersex*.[10] Here, the rabbi and Talmud scholar places intersex readings of rabbinic texts in ways that both contribute to high scholarship and, as in her contribution to this volume, will be exciting for activists and nonspecialists.

After the period of creativity in Jewish lesbian publishing in the late twentieth century and the silence of the past few decades, these recent works indicate a renewed interest in Jewish lesbian, queer, intersex, and trans feminist issues. These works are complementary to each other, and

Jewcy will be the first book in this regenerating field to focus on lesbian and women's experience with multiple genders and in a queer way. We hope that this book will also be able to reach a more expansive readership. *Jewcy* purposely brings together older and younger contributors, and also those with more experience in publishing and those with less. Reflecting the lived experience of the Jewish feminist queer habitus today, *Jewcy* combines accessible scholarly chapters with more literary styles including memoir, poetry, oral history, and spoken word. Some of these styles are relatively traditional, while others are alternative and experimental.

Jewcy stands on the shoulders of the important historical figures in Jewish lesbian writing and also reintroduces some historical works and writers to contemporary readers. This volume presents the most comprehensive analyses in Jewish lesbian queer studies to date. The chapters span an array of genres. Together, they present the vivid diversity of Jewish lesbian feminists as well as of Jewish queer lesbian feminist scholarship today, including fresh interdisciplinary offerings. This collection makes an innovative contribution to Jewish studies; lesbian and queer studies; women's and gender studies; theology and religion; literature; oral history, politics, sociology, and anthropology; and racial, ethnic, Indigenous, and cultural diversity studies. We share accessible and incisive scholarship, memoir, poetry, spoken word, and midrash (a distinctive form of Jewish storytelling based on the Hebrew Bible). As such, *Jewcy* contains both academic and more popular analyses of ancient Jewish texts relevant for contemporary issues; poetry and scholarship on poetry, including both historical and contemporary; memoir from senior and younger Jewish lesbians; and experimental new forms that cross and defy genre. The work includes authors and subjects with stated Jewish lesbian identities and an array of additional contributors. In bringing them together we hope to model new modes of community building where identity need not be policed at the entryway. Similarly, the project offers perspectives by and on a range of Jewish ethnicities, including African American, Northern European (US) American, Indigenous, Ashkenazi, Sephardi, and Mizrahi. Moreover, at a time when fewer Jewish families are exclusively Jewish, the book offers visions from contributors of mixed heritage, such as contributors who are Jewish and Muslim, Jewish and Kurdish, and Jewish and Chamoru. We hope that the vivacity and multifaceted diversity of *Jewcy* will help launch a significant reorientation of the field and among activists to one deeply grounded in diversity.

Chapter Briefs

We begin with a complex work by an amazing new writer. In "Henna Night Dyke," this mixed Albanian, Turkish, Muslim, and Ashkenazi Jewish thinker and activist explores the push and pull of her multicultural heritages, her peoples, and her changing self to create new communities to remind us that "traditions start when someone makes a new one" as she imagines herself as part of a first generation of henna night dykes.

Next, we have Sarra Lev's "Deconstructing the Binary, or Not? On a Discourse of Intersex in Early Rabbinic Literature." Unlike much current practice, which erases intersex bodies from the landscape through surgery, scattered throughout rabbinic literature are references to an *androginos* and a *tumtum*—one who has both male and female genitals and one whose genitals are decisively one or the other but are somehow concealed. The ancient, early rabbis had multiple approaches to understanding how intersex bodies fit into their otherwise-binary sex and gender system. This chapter, addressed to both the scholar and layperson, explores one of those approaches, which appears in the most elaborate treatment of intersex in this literature, the second chapter of Tosefta Bikkurim.

Following these first two pieces is "At the Intersection of Sephardic, Mizrahi, and LGBTQ+: The Story of a Community Emerging out of the Margins," by Ruben Shimonov and Marielle Tawil. In this article, the authors describe the origin and development of the Sephardic Mizrahi Q Network (SMQN)—a one-of-a-kind organization serving LGBTQ+ Sephardic and Mizrahi Jews, a less-represented segment of the Jewish population. Written by the founding executive director and a board member of the organization with the participation of various community members, the chapter is part oral history and part ethnography. It shares SMQN's community-building approach, core values, and theory of change as it tells the story of the growth of SMQN. This story serves as a remarkable case study in social innovation and community leadership. The authors argue that it is imperative to elevate stories of intersectional Jewish communities on the periphery. Lifting up and highlighting these experiences not only empowers these marginalized communities but also deepens our collective understanding of the rich diversity and mosaic of the Jewish people.

Vinny Calvo Prell's chapter examines identity policing, internalized oppression, and making space for difference. For this piece, he focuses on the dynamics of exclusion that can happen in the lesbian community as we often erase one another for the sake of purity of identity. A Chamoru

Jew, Calvo Prell brings her own experiences of not feeling Jewish enough or "of color" enough to bear in her analysis. Calvo Prell argues that such dynamics both harm us as individuals and limit our collective political efficacy.

Lauren Hakimi offers a provocative read on the controversial Chelly Wilson, a Sephardi and Ladino-speaking Greek Jew from Salonika. Wilson was a lesbian who is noted to have loved the second of her two husbands. Raised orthodox, Wilson was a porn-theater owner who'd managed to leave Athens weeks after World War II broke out. She was also one of the creators of gay porn in the US. Wilson has recently been reintroduced to the public as an inspiring figure, but Hakimi also wonders if there might be other, less savory lessons to learn from this foremother.

Yeshiva University's Joy Ladin shares with us new poems. "Anniversaries" is a sequence of four love poems to her wife written "as gifts for one of our two wedding anniversaries—the public wedding, which took place in August, or the private ceremony held on the stoop of Emily Dickinson's house in January—for the years 2018 through 2022, years during which my health declined precipitously due to an incurable and largely untreatable illness. The poems reflect the counterpoint between our joy in one another and my increasing disability, and the love that encompasses both."

In "The Sephardic Palimpsests of Emma Lazarus," Leonard Stein explores an intersectional expression in the literary career of Emma Lazarus, the nineteenth-century Jewish (US) American poet and activist. Reading, translating, and rewriting Hebrew literature from medieval Spain afforded Lazarus, a Sephardic Jew, an ancestral literary heritage for writing about same-sex desire, especially as reflected in Andalusian conventions of homoeroticism. Lazarus's reliance on previous German translations, in addition to the appropriation of medieval texts in her original homoerotic poetry, produces literary palimpsests that help bridge layers of time and space between a medieval homeland and a modern diasporic identity.

Sabrina Sojourner offers us her innovative "Remembering Sinai: A Spoken-Word Midrash." Here, Sojourner provides a midrash on the biblical primary source Sh'mot/Exodus 6:1–20:23. Sojourner's beautiful work in this piece is a complex project incorporating Jewish identity, feminism, race, queerness, spoken-word poetics, and midrash.

A. S. Hakkâri further opens up the field with "Life on the Borderlands: Mizrahiut, Transfemininity, and Stateless Diasporas." In this work, Mizrahi, Kurdish, and trans female author Hakkâri develops Jewish, transfeminist, and Mizrahi borderland theorizing. Most writers view these identities as distinct narrative lenses through which one can read a life, but for Hakkâri each of these disparate selves can exist only in relation to the others, and any attempt to extricate them from one another leaves behind a mess. Only by taking these aspects of herself together as a broader whole can she begin to uncover a helpful and unifying experience among them. These identities exist in the borderlands of their communities. This leaves them—Hakkâri, and others with similar identities— stranded from their communities and seeking support with difficulty, despite fully sharing the experience every one of those communities has of hatred and marginalization.

"Meeting Cicely, or Love and Politics: A Black Jewish Lesbian Memoir" is an excerpt Carol Conaway prepared for this volume from her political memoir-in-progress. In it, she examines her experiences as an African American lesbian living her dream of becoming a Jew. The chapter focuses on her 1973 move from Philadelphia to Boston just as racial unrest in the city reached an apex. Conaway shares her challenges as a Black Jewish lesbian at the time with a telling of the racism she faced, particularly in a group of professional and educated lesbians. Despite the racism in the group generally, it was there that Conaway met the woman who would become her lifelong partner and with whom she would navigate a relationship as a Black Jew partnered with a white non-Jew. With exquisite sensitivity, Conaway deftly brings readers along into her initial naïveté about the prejudices she encountered in response to her combination of gender, race, class, sexual orientation, and mental illness.

Marla Brettschneider's "Leslie Feinberg's Complex Jewish Lesbian Feminism" analyzes Leslie Feinberg's writing, activism, life, and political commitments within a Jewish context. Scholarship on Feinberg often overlooks her Jewish identity and its role in her work. Centering Jewishness, we can interrupt this silencing and better understand Feinberg and the histories of progressive movements. Given the complexity of Feinberg's focus, the analysis brings gender, sexuality, class, and race and their very multiplicity into relief as related inherently to their justice politics. The chapter situates each aspect of his identity and justice politics in the Jewish historical context of his time and place. From this, Brettschneider concludes that while we should appreciate the radicalness of her signal contribution, we should also recognize Feinberg as relatively aligned with US Jewry.

We close the volume with Rona Matlow's "Postmodern Concepts of Sex, Gender, and Sexuality in the Framework of the Jewish Lesbian." This work explores the concepts of sex and gender, starting with biblical and rabbinic texts and then moving on to contemporary analytic frameworks. Here Matlow shows that sex and gender are not, and never have been, binary. These constructs have been misconstrued by society for millennia. Once the author has reframed sex and gender as nonbinary, the work then shifts focus to the language of sexuality, where Matlow explores the perspectives of Jewish lesbians and how to define that group from a standpoint that incorporates a new framework of nonbinary gender.

Notes

1. Rebecca T. Alpert and Marla Brettschneider, "Lesbianism," *Shalvi/Hyman Encyclopedia of Jewish Women*, updated June 23, 2021, https://jwa.org/encyclopedia/article/lesbianism.

2. Carol P. Christ and Judith Plaskow, eds., *Womanspirit Rising: A Feminist Reader in Religion* (San Francisco: Harper Collins, 1979); see also Judith Plaskow, "Blaming the Jews for the Birth of Patriarchy," in *Nice Jewish Girls: A Lesbian Anthology*, ed. Evelyn Torton Beck (Watertown, MA: Persephone Press, 1982), 250–54.

3. For a more detailed history of these periods and fields, readers may be interested in Marla Brettschneider, "Jewish Lesbians: Contemporary Activism and Its Challenges," in *Jewish Women's History from Antiquity to the Present*, ed. Federica Francesconi and Rebecca Lynn Winer, 419–40 (Detroit: Wayne State University Press, 2021).

4. See Marla Brettschneider, "Jewish Lesbians: New Work in the Field," introduction to *Journal of Lesbian Studies* special issue, ed. Marla Brettschneider, 23, no. 1 (2019): 2–20, which was dedicated to the memory of Melanie Kaye/Kantrowitz.

5. Marla Brettschneider, ed., *Jewish Lesbian Scholarship in a Time of Change* (London: Routledge, 2023).

6. Joy Ladin, *The Soul of the Stranger: Reading God and Torah from a Transgender Perspective* (Waltham, MA: Brandeis University Press, 2018).

7. Elena Dykewomon and Judith Katz, eds., *To Be a Jewish Dyke in the 21st Century*, special issue of *Sinister Wisdom* 119 (Winter 2021).

8. Jane Litman and Jakob Hero-Shaw, eds., *Liberating Gender for Jews and Allies: The Wisdom of Transkeit* (Newcastle upon Tyne, UK: Cambridge Scholars Publishing, 2022).

9. Max Strassfeld, *Trans Talmud: Androgynes and Eunuchs in Rabbinic Literature* (Oakland: University of California Press, 2022).

10. Sarra Lev, *And the Sages Did Not Know: Early Rabbinic Approaches to Intersex* (Philadelphia: University of Pennsylvania Press, forthcoming).

References

Alpert, Rebecca T., and Marla Brettschneider. "Lesbianism." *Shalvi/Hyman Encyclopedia of Jewish Women*, updated June 23, 2021. https://jwa.org/encyclopedia/article/lesbianism.

Brettschneider, Marla, editor. *Jewish Lesbian Scholarship in a Time of Change*. London: Routledge, 2023.

———. "Jewish Lesbians: Contemporary Activism and Its Challenges." In *Jewish Women's History from Antiquity to the Present*, edited by Federica Francesconi and Rebecca Lynn Winer, 419–40. Detroit: Wayne State University Press, 2021.

———. "Jewish Lesbians: New Work in the Field." Introduction to *Journal of Lesbian Studies* special issue, edited by Marla Brettschneider, 23, no. 1 (2019): 2–20.

Christ, Carol P., and Judith Plaskow, editors. *Womanspirit Rising: A Feminist Reader in Religion*. San Francisco: Harper Collins, 1979.

Dykewomon, Elena, and Judith Katz, editors. *To Be a Jewish Dyke in the 21st Century*. Special issue of *Sinister Wisdom* 119 (Winter 2021).

Ladin, Joy. *The Soul of the Stranger: Reading God and Torah from a Transgender Perspective*. Waltham, MA: Brandeis University Press, 2018.

Lev, Sarra. *And the Sages Did Not Know: Early Rabbinic Approaches to Intersex*. Philadelphia: University of Pennsylvania Press, forthcoming.

Litman, Jane, and Jakob Hero-Shaw, editors. *Liberating Gender for Jews and Allies: The Wisdom of Transkeit*. Newcastle upon Tyne, UK: Cambridge Scholars Publishing, 2022.

Plaskow, Judith. "Blaming the Jews for the Birth of Patriarchy." In *Nice Jewish Girls: A Lesbian Anthology*, edited by Evelyn Torton Beck, 250–54. Watertown, MA: Persephone Press, 1982.

Strassfeld, Max. *Trans Talmud: Androgynes and Eunuchs in Rabbinic Literature*. Oakland: University of California Press, 2022.

Chapter 1

Henna Night Dyke

ANONYMOUS

Albanian ladies appear to be even more addicted than Osmanlis to the use of cosmetics. . . . No sooner are they married than they begin to dye their hair with a decoction made from gall-nuts and palm oil, stain their eyelashes with antimony, and extend their eyebrows till they meet over the nose. . . . [They redden] their lips and cheeks with cochineal or carmine, while their nails and the palms of their hands are liberally stained . . . with henna.

—*Balkan Home-Life*, 1917, Lucy M. J. Garnett

My cousin and I were going to get in trouble if her dad came into the room and smelled the nail polish we were using. I wasn't sure why. Something about wearing nail polish felt sexual, but only because the forbidden was usually sexual. At least, it felt that way on the Muslim side of my family. At this point, I was still visiting my cousins regularly, and we went to weddings and holidays. By the time I was in my early teens, most of those things had stopped happening. Or maybe we stopped getting invited.

On my dad's side, I always felt like I was getting mixed messages. The same people who didn't want us painting our nails would also give us (the young girls) sparkly accessories or undergarments as gifts. It felt like there was an invisible, always-moving line of self-expression we couldn't cross but also couldn't find. That was less the case for weddings, where everyone was wearing heavy makeup and high heels, and it wasn't a big deal. In fact, it was encouraged. I once got in trouble with my dad for wearing flats to a wedding, knowing that my dress was long enough to cover my feet and that I couldn't take the pain of those heels for the full night of dancing that awaited.

Weddings and circumcisions were huge occasions on my Muslim side, and on my Jewish side I don't remember a single one happening at all. In my Muslim family, these events were frequent enough that you could use them as an opportunity to get together. I loved the loud music; the flying dollar bills; glittering, swirling women; circle dances; and beating drums. Whether or not the food was good, the company and dancing always were. Back in the village, I was told, weddings could be a week-long affair, and brides would receive special, sequined makeup applied using lightly wetted soap as a tacky glue. Then and now, it's a time of high stress, high fashion, and serious pampering. Typical wedding gifts among Muslims and Jews from my dad's region still include lace-edged towels and luxurious soaps.

Still, my mom thought the whole thing was shallow, and I often felt ashamed due to my love of makeup and fashion—like I couldn't be smart and enjoy those things. My dad often yelled at me if I wore makeup that was too visible or clothes he didn't like. Cosplay, historical costuming, and makeup felt like more things I loved that were another "line" that I didn't understand. "A wedding is one day of your life," my mom told me. "Grades are forever."

Back when I dated guys, I imagined my wedding would be a chance to be accepted and have my families come together. I felt like I would go into the wedding an awkward girl and come out the other side beautiful and graceful forever, like a living photograph, and that no one would have a problem with me for how I did or didn't look anymore. I would get to feel special. That I was loved, or wanted, would become unimpeachable.

Realizing I was gay in practice and in theory meant reimagining all of it and realizing how many faces I wouldn't see there. I struggled to fit my gayness into the paradigms of American friends whose families had been here for many more generations than my dad's had. Sometimes, I feel guilty for wanting acceptance in my dad's family, like I'm proving that Muslims are homophobic—while also being an assimilationist traitor to some radical queer cause for wanting to participate in the parts of my culture that reify heterosexuality, or whatever. I keep trying to explain to people that it's not like I can cut my dad off. It's a different culture than is mainstream for LGBTQ+ Americans. Talking to my dad without this part of me being accepted feels like a future catastrophe I'm always putting off—always holding my breath.

I'm still struggling to shake this gaze that's telling me that the makeup I wear is too much or too little, that hates the clothes I wear, that thinks I look like shit or a bimbo or a moron, that thinks I'm destroying or dishonoring my family. Sometimes I worry that I'm confirming people's bad feelings about Jews or Muslims in my communities "marrying out" depending on the first impression I give them, even if clothes didn't feel like as big of a deal on my mom's side of the family.

Growing up, the message I received was that the cultural values and aesthetics of my dad's family were at odds with being a Jew. I was still getting rejected in Jewish spaces, and I wasn't raised with a Jewish education. Persistently communicated to me was that I had to be one thing or the other—literally, the Other. More than anything, I really wanted to hold onto the traditions of my dad's side and get to be a Jew while I practiced them. I was sick of being told they weren't Jewish.

Reading about the histories and cultures of Jews in my dad's region meant confronting the antisemitism I'd grown up with in our community. But it also meant seeing commonalities that started to stitch closed the wounds inside myself. The Jews brushing elbows with my dad's family wore similar clothes, ate mostly the same foods, had henna nights, traded goods in the same bustling villages and cities, and had the same lace-trimmed towels in their wedding chests. Spoke the same languages, drank the same raki. For them, being a Jew meant doing and being those things while carrying on a philosophy and way of life that I identified with. My first Pride event was an all-LGBTQ Sefaradi-Mizrahi Shabbat dinner. Suddenly, floating between my families' identities felt less like a burden and more like a skill. And my time with the organization that hosted the Shabbat dinner? It felt like a blessing.

In Jewish spaces, fellowships, and even online groups focused on Sefaradi and LGBTQ+ Jewish histories, you find people talking about people like themselves who have existed in history. Jewish women who loved other women, Jews who made an exodus from one gender to another, Jews who led colorful lives in music (Roza Eskenazi and Flory Jagoda) in the Balkans and Anatolia. People are always talking about ancestors, ancestors, ancestors and what they wanted and didn't want. I feel like I can't profess to know or infer what my ancestors wanted. When I think about them, I feel shame. They must be disappointed in me. My face just burns.

In my most secret heart, I imagine ancestors on both sides of my family who might have had the same inclinations as me but didn't exist during a time and place where they could pursue those feelings. That, too, feels like a violation—feels like I'm going too far. But in my heart I want to believe they existed. I want to believe we existed.

My Jewish job sent me honey for the new year, and I put it in a honey pot given to me by one of my Muslim aunts. Here I am, in a strange wedding dance with life, of which I am slowly learning the steps, that I cannot stop. I don't know whether I'll be able to participate in every tradition that my peers will. But I know that traditions start when someone makes a new one. All I know is that I have to live. I don't know any other way but this one. I love whom I love, and I am what I am, and, God willing, I am what I will be.

Maybe I'll be part of the first generation of henna night dykes.

Chapter 2

Deconstructing the Binary, or Not?

On a Discourse of Intersex in Early Rabbinic Literature

SARRA LEV

This chapter is about intersex in early rabbinic literature. With reference to that literature, the term *intersex* refers to persons (or nonhuman animals) born with variant genitals—genitals that do not readily conform to the category "male" or "female."[1] The rabbis refer to a person with (what they see as) a combination of male and female genitals as an *androginos*, a word made up of the Greek words for man and woman. What, you might ask, does intersex in rabbinic literature have to do with Jewish lesbians? Well, for me, quite a bit. I am a Jewish lesbian (albeit nonbinary), and I study and teach rabbinic literature. When I came out in the 1980s, there was almost nothing written about Jewish lesbians. Certainly, no one at that time had mined rabbinic literature for sources that described who I am and where I fit into my traditional texts. The desire to find those sources led me to texts on sex, sexuality, and gender. Few were about lesbians, but some were about bodies that did not fit into the mold of binary sex and gender. I wanted to understand more, so I began learning about intersex.

In this chapter, I scrutinize the structure and the contents of the seminal text (pun intended) on intersex in early rabbinic literature—Tosefta Bikkurim 2:4–7. My goal here is twofold. First, in the bulk of this essay, I argue that Seder Androginos both deconstructs and fortifies the rabbinic male/female sex and gender (hereafter sex/gender) binary, sometimes simultaneously. That the rabbis recognize the very notion of intersex seems to be an affirming move, but through my analysis I demonstrate that all is not as it seems. An *androginos*'s turf in the rabbinic sex/gender system can be a difficult place to occupy.

Second, I suggest using the dissenting minority opinion of Rabbi Yose as an entry point to imagining a worthier place. The rulings that take up most of this chapter represent the majority opinion of the rabbis. But Seder Androginos ends with Rabbi Yose's opinion, which I will argue can open a door to a different worldview. I end this essay by considering how Rabbi Yose might push us towards something new, something that moves beyond what we ourselves know.

As with all issues connected with identity politics, it is complicated for someone who is not intersex themselves to speak about intersex. All the more so, I want to acknowledge that I enter difficult territory by writing a paper that explores intersex as it relates to the binary sex/gender matrix. Many intersex activists have no interest in querying the sex/gender binary and justifiably decry the use of their bodies to deconstruct the binary sex/gender matrix;[2] nobody wants to be used for someone else's agenda. Some, however, do state that project as *one of* their goals.[3] To be sure, my experience as a nonbinary lesbian cannot be compared to that of an intersex person. However, some lesbians (especially of my generation) and some intersex people share an intimacy with the closet and the experience of searching for a history in which they are acknowledged. Although neither lesbians nor intersex people are recognized as *participating in* this ancient conversation, I hope this essay may breathe life into one small shard of that history—one that finds its voice in rabbinic literature.[4]

Let us begin!

In her article "Queer Cut Bodies," Morgan Holmes describes in some detail the genital surgery that was inflicted upon her seven-year-old body. Cutting away at her "enlarged" clitoris, the doctors left Holmes with "one-half centimeter of glans, which was then pushed backward into the surrounding flesh and sutured down."[5] Holmes informs us that this is typical of the surgery to which intersex children are regularly subjected. But, as she points out, surgery is only one manifestation of a more fundamental issue. To make her point, Holmes expands on Anne Fausto-Sterling's remark that "hermaphrodites have unruly bodies. They do not fall into a binary classification: only a surgical shoehorn can put them there."[6] Holmes continues, "While it is true that it is a surgical shoehorn that engenders the intersexual, this process occurs in tandem with a larger ideological shoehorn of a sex/gender binary. What the treatment of inter-sexed children underscores is that we are all forced to conform to specific, binarized, heteronormative gender roles."[7]

What would a world that was not built on that shoehorn see when it looked at intersex genitals? Holmes responds to an article in the gay and lesbian journal *XTRA* that describes her as having been "born with the genitalia of both men and women" by saying, "I was not born with the genitalia of both men and women; I was born with child-sized inter-sexed genitals."[8] As Holmes explains, in a world not organized around binary sex and gender, her interviewer would not have needed to describe intersex genitals in this fashion because an intelligible vocabulary would already exist for that description. Indeed, Holmes wonders "what the potential might be for the proclamation 'It's an intersexual!'" in a birth announcement.[9]

In 1993, the biologist Anne Fausto-Sterling, in an article enti-tled "The Five Sexes: Why Male and Female Are Not Enough," wrote, "Western culture is deeply committed to the idea that there are only two sexes. . . . But if the state and the legal system have an interest in main-taining a two-party sexual system, they are in defiance of nature. For biologically speaking, there are many gradations running from female to male; and depending on how one calls the shots, one can argue that along that spectrum lie at least five sexes—and perhaps even more."[10]

Fausto-Sterling's article was groundbreaking. It addressed scientifi-cally what gender theorists like Judith Butler had addressed only theoret-ically—the mutability and indeterminacy of the categories of biological sex. Simply put, these theorists claimed that the hierarchical binary male/female is a social construction rather than a natural given—not only the hierarchy, but the very fact of those categories. These theorists believed that disrupting the binary would also disrupt the hierarchy that was inher-ent in it. Fausto-Sterling's work supported that claim, basing itself on actual bodies that broke through the male/female binary—intersex bodies. In her book *Sexing the Body*, she harshly critiques western culture for eradicating all signs of sexes that defy the categories *male* and *female*, giv-ing "the two-sex system . . . the appearance of being both inborn and nat-ural. . . . Moreover, modern surgical techniques help maintain the two-sex system. Today children who are born 'either/or—neither/both'—a fairly common phenomenon—usually disappear from view because doctors 'correct' them right away with surgery."[11]

Rabbinic culture, too, is heavily invested in the categories *male* and *female*, distinguishing at length between the precepts that men must follow and those that women must follow. Nevertheless, unlike what Fausto-Sterling describes, an *androginos*—someone that the rabbis perceive as born with male and female genitals[12]—is often discussed in the rabbinic period. The primary early rabbinic text on this subject appears in the Tosefta, one of the main collections from the early rabbinic period, which is the first two centuries CE. Our text (hereafter, Seder Androginos[13]) opens:

An *androginos* is
in some ways, like[14] men,
and in some ways, like women,
and in some ways, like men and women,
and in some ways, like neither men nor women.[15]

Let me briefly situate us geographically and historically. Most scholars agree that the Tosefta is (loosely defined) a collection of Palestinian sources, many of them legal, that were not included in the more well-known work of the same period, the Mishnah. Scholars believe that the Tosefta was redacted later than the Mishnah in the third century and that later material inevitably crept in, though they also believe that some of its contents are older than Mishnaic texts. The most recent scholarly consensus is that the early rabbis did not wield tremendous influence as a group. Still, it is likely that the opinions of specific individuals among them held sway locally, in their own communities. Palestine was under Roman rule at this time. Life under the Romans during these two centuries varied according to which emperor was ruling and what regulations local governors imposed on the population at any given moment. Jewish uprisings and outright rebellions punctuated the two centuries, a sign of plain discontent, but even so, Greco-Roman culture played a pervasive role in the lives of Jews at that time.[16]

As for the prevailing attitude toward intersex in the Roman world, the response to the question of how an *androginos*'s body might fit into society in both Greek and Roman early antiquity was uncomplicated and brutal. Sources indicate that until the beginning of the Roman Empire, like other unwanted children, infants with atypical genitalia were "exposed" or drowned.[17] With the rise of the Roman Empire, the practice of killing a newborn *androginos* ended, although *androginoi* were still treated as "freaks."[18]

Later sources show that there were attempts to integrate those with atypical genitals into the legal system, albeit differently from rabbinic law.[19] Several legal references appear in Justinian's Digest (compiled in the sixth century CE), including an edict by the Roman jurist Ulpian (who wrote in the beginning of the third century CE): "With whom is a hermaphrodite comparable? I rather think each one should be ascribed to that sex which is prevalent in his or her make-up."[20]

I want to be clear that any direct comparison or contrast with this Roman legal material is impossible. While we can speak of the two-century span that early rabbinic materials cover, it is impossible to precisely or even approximately date the individual texts within this span. Thus, it is impossible to know when in these two centuries this text was written (and whether it was during a period of relative calm or significant upheaval), not to mention what the climate was concerning sex and gender in general and intersexuality in particular. The prospect that a future historian might contextualize the Broadway show *Hamilton* by explaining that it was written sometime between 1825 and 2025 illustrates just how inexact our historical contextualization of these texts can be.

The Toseftan text quoted above is immediately followed by a series of four passages. These break down the categories men, women, both, and neither into a list of halakhot dictating the circumstances under which an *androginos* must behave or be treated according to each.[21] The Tosefta's only explicit concern is with what today's gender theorists call gendered performance. The Tosefta's authors prescribed gendered behavior through halakhot in areas of purity, inheritance, relationships, personal appearance, the fulfillment of mitzvot, and other day-to-day issues. The text explicitly engages the question of how a person who does not fit into the accepted binary categories of male and female must perform their gender, making it one of the constitutive texts constructing gender in the early rabbinic world. Nowhere is there an attempt to deny the existence of *androginoi* or to assign them exclusively to the category of male or female. In fact, Fausto-Sterling herself uses the Tosefta as an example of gender multiplicity, writing, "Jewish religious texts such as the . . . Tosefta list extensive regulations for people of mixed sex . . . Judaic law provided a means for integrating hermaphrodites [*sic*] into mainstream culture."[22]

We need to ask, however, Does the fact that the Tosefta does not classify these bodies solely as male or female indicate a more expansive understanding of gender, as Fausto-Sterling claims, or does the Tosefta's discourse also reinforce the gender binary to which she objects? I investigate this question through an examination of the overall structure of these halakhot and through some of their details and claim that, in some ways, the answer to this question reflects the text itself. There are ways in which this text defies the binary, ways in which it reinforces it, ways in which it does both, and ways in which it does neither. I begin at the end, with the final category: ways in which the text neither reinforces nor deconstructs the gender binary—in other words, ways in which this text is not exactly (or at least not *only*) about gender, even while it is.

Ways in Which the Text Neither Reinforces nor Deconstructs the Gender Binary

Although Seder Androginos seems to be all about gender, let's examine it from a different angle for a moment; let us say, that is, that it is actually engaged in a much broader rabbinic question: What do we do when something (or, in our case, someone) doesn't quite fit into our predefined categories? While the rabbis cared about the practical day-to-day reality, they were equally (if not more) committed to the purely theoretical project of thinking. As Jacob Neusner has pointed out, "The Mishnaic mode of thought is to . . . deal with gray areas and to lay down principles for disposing of cases of doubt."[23]

Indeed, one need not look further than the opening of this very chapter of Tosefta to understand this better. There, the rabbis raise an almost identical issue about a *koy*,[24] an animal that is sometimes classified as wild, sometimes as domesticated, sometimes as both, and sometimes as neither. Not only is the idea of this hybrid animal similar to that of an *androginos*,[25] but the language and structure of the discussion are directly parallel. Clearly, this text is an exploration of the limits of gender categories not as a unique subject but as one more manifestation of the ever-repeating conversation about classification and its limitations.

Whether or not the text is meant to actively construct gender, however, that is certainly its effect, and, unlike with the *koy*, the discussion about *androginoi* has real-life implications for people—people whom the rabbis seem to have known existed.[26] The rest of this chapter, therefore, will be devoted to exploring how gender is ultimately constructed within the text and what its implications are for intersex people, whether or not these questions are reflected in the text's original intent.

Ways in Which the Text Deconstructs the Binary

It is possible, at first glance, to see the overall structure of Seder Androginos as defying the binary system, beginning with that binary and building intentionally toward a more flexible understanding of gender. The chapter does first place an *androginos* into traditional binary categories, outlining ways in which they are male and ways in which they are female. From there, however, the chapter unfurls the possibility that an *androginos* is, in fact, both. This leaves us with the notion that there are only two genders but establishes that one could perform as both rather than being confined to one or the other. The next step presumably takes us out of the binary altogether, placing an *androginos* into the category of "neither," allowing that there is another option outside of those two categories. Finally, the chapter ends with Rabbi Yose's minority opinion[27] that an *androginos* is *beriah l'atzmo*—a creation sui generis, creating a class that is presumably entirely outside the binary gender system.

By creating categories in which an *androginos* is both male and female or neither male nor female, the anonymous majority[28] submits that there are situations in which one must forgo the binary. What does it mean to be both male and female? What does it mean to be neither? Whether or not the rabbis had this in mind, this framing immediately raises these questions before one even begins to explore the implications of the halakhot that follow. That the listener would likely ask these questions already sets in motion the possibility of a nonbinary reading of gender.

It is not only the creation of the two categories "both" and "neither" but the fact that an *androginos* drifts between these four categories that calls into question the static nature of the sex/gender binary. If it is possible to be all these things, then there is clearly a sex option that is not merely male or female. This seems to be what Fausto-Sterling is getting at when she states that "Judaic law provided a means *for integrating hermaphrodites into mainstream culture*" (italics mine).

But before we are convinced of rabbinic tradition's openness to sex/gender elasticity or to seeing sex on a spectrum, it is essential to understand what this "integration" of intersex people into mainstream culture looked like. While it is true that the Tosefta does not shy away from admitting the existence of possibilities that defy binary sex and gender, just what are the implications of the fact that the rabbis regularly discuss *androginoi*? Might this recognition, at the same time, serve to reify the existing binary? For this, I turn to the ways in which the text reinforces the gender binary.

Ways in Which the Text Reinforces the Binary

I have noted that the existence of the categories "both" and "neither" and the fact that an *androginos* travels *among* these four categories indicate a move away from the sex/gender binary. However, the fact that the categories of male and female are what guides these halakhot turns us back to the binary. That all four categories reference the categories male and female offers us no real options outside of the gender binary itself. Nowhere is an alternative to male or female named, except negatively as a lack of either or as an excess of them (I discuss Rabbi Yose's opinion in the next section).

By turning to the individual halakhot that appear in the various gender boxes, we also see the tendency to reify the binary. The governing principle in determining which of the four categories an *androginos* will belong to at any given moment is what I call the precautionary principle. This (often-unspoken) rule is based on the question, What contingencies must be put in place when considering what transgression might occur if, heaven forbid, . . . ? The majority opinion in Seder Androginos is most often concerned with the sex/gender-specific halakhot that an *androginos* might transgress if we consider them male, on the one hand, or female, on the other.

Consider, for example, the laws of seclusion, which forbid a man and a woman from being alone with each other. In Seder Androginos, an *androginos* is forbidden from being alone with women, lest they are "really" a man. Likewise, they are prohibited from being alone with men, lest they are "really" a woman. This classic rabbinic principle can be applied to many of the halakhot in Seder Androginos.[29]

If most of the categorization in this chapter of the Tosefta merely averts the transgression of halakhot that are incumbent upon each (binary) sex, what underlies Seder Androginos is binary sex and gender. That is to say, an *androginos* sometimes falls into the "neither male nor female" section and sometimes into the "both male and female" section because the rabbis understand an *androginos* as *either* male or female. Thus, there is an ongoing effort to preserve binary sex/gender, always keeping in mind that an *androginos* may be capable of transgressing as both a male and a female simultaneously—reifying the intransigent categories of male and female.

Ways in Which the Text Both Reinforces and Deconstructs the Gender Binary

We have established that the text defies the binary in some ways and reinforces it in others. In this section, I "read against the grain," examining internal contradictions in the text to show that in some ways, the text does both simultaneously—reinforcing the binary while deconstructing it. Here, I will argue that even that which falls into the binary sex/gender system that the authors of this text work so hard to preserve is merely a house of cards.

Let us look again at the halakhot that I examine above. Tosefta Bikkurim 2:4 states that, like a man, an *androginos* may not be alone with women. Indeed, it seems logical that this halakhah appears with "ways in which an *androginos* is like a man." However, the next halakhah states that an *androginos* may not be alone with men, like a woman. Again, taken alone, this halakhah logically appears with "ways in which an *androginos* is like a woman." In effect, however, the combination of these two halakhot leaves an *androginos* unable to be alone with men or women. Within the laws regarding seclusion, therefore, an *androginos* is, in fact, neither like a man nor like a woman! The rabbis could as readily have written, "an *androginos* may be alone with neither women nor men," and inserted this halakhah into the category "ways in which an *androginos* is neither like men nor like women." They chose, however, to present an *androginos* as falling directly into the binary, first as a man, and then as a woman. The text thus leads us astray in its attempt to reify the binary by placing an *androginos* into these two binary categories. Seder Androginos employs this same technique in several other halakhot as well, including inheritance and purity laws. In each case, it places an *androginos* into the category of "like a man" first and "like a woman" second, while, objectively, they end up like neither.

The category "ways in which an *androginos* is like both" also exposes the rabbinic house of cards. Consider this list: One may not damage or kill them; they may eat of the holy food permitted to both men and women; their mother must bring a sacrifice to atone for her impurity when they are born as she would if she gave birth to either a boy or a girl.[30] One notices quickly that much of the category "both male and female" is in fact, in the main, genderless. One could easily have said "ways in which an *androginos* is considered a (rabbinic) Jew"![31] Nowhere does the text claim, for example, that an *androginos* must (or even may) dress in the clothes of both men and women or marry a woman *and* a man. Moreover, as Max Strassfeld has pointed out, "Despite the fact that the injury of the *androginos* would seem to pose a 'universal' category of human rights, this universality is still framed through the poles of gender dichotomy. To belong, the *androginos* must be like men and women in order to qualify."[32]

Finally, and perhaps most importantly, we must examine even those places that tend toward the nonbinary not only for their ability to expand our understanding of sex and gender but for what that broader understanding will produce. Does the prospect of a rabbinic "third" sex/gender or "sex/gender continuum" build itself in the image of the two gendered system? Does it introduce alternatives into the system while retaining the hierarchy of the binary?

We see this again through the deceptive categorization discussed above. The accumulation of halakhot regarding an *androginos* leaves an intersex person in a position that is truly like neither a man nor a woman. This does not mean, however, that they have escaped all gendered categorization and may find their way in a less rigid system. Instead, they are stranded in a system that is entirely dependent on sex for its obligations and privileges—an *androginos* bears most of the obligations of both men and women and few of the privileges of either (though they may find themselves more privileged than women in some cases). While a woman may be alone with other women and a man with other men, an *androginos* may be alone with neither. Similarly, while a male receives an inheritance after a parent's death and a female receives *mezonot* (limited sustenance), an *androginos* may receive nothing. Is an *androginos*, then, truly integrated?

The crowning glory of this series of halakhot is the minority opinion of Rabbi Yose: "an *androginos* is a *beriah l'atzmo* [a creation sui generis] and the sages could not determine whether they are male or female."[33]

Again, Rabbi Yose's statement initially seems like an antidote to a binary system. "No," he says, "an *androginos* is not sometimes male, sometimes female, sometimes both, and sometimes neither! An *androginos* is a creation sui generis. We cannot classify them in these binary terms!" Surely, this statement is the salvation of the sex/gender continuum.

Once again, however, while Rabbi Yose offers us an alternative, his alternative cannot help but be steeped in the rhetoric of the binary. While he opens with the statement "an *androginos* is a creation sui generis," he finishes his sentence with the words "and the sages could not decide whether they are a man or a woman." No sooner has he freed us from the binary than he himself returns to it. Rather than name a new category of gender, he claims instead that the sages could not *decide* to which of the two binary genders—man and woman—they should relegate an *androginos*. As Strassfeld argues, Rabbi Yose does not negate the reading of the majority but colludes in their centralization of gender as an organizing category.[34]

Even if we are to understand Rabbi Yose as opposing the sages, his opinion leaves us in a state of dis-ease—not knowing what to do *halakhically* with his statement. While the sages offer us concrete halakhot in many categories, Rabbi Yose offers no practical application of his position. Should an *androginos* be obligated in only those commandments incumbent upon all people? Is the impurity of an *androginos* not to be considered impurity at all? Or should they avoid contact with sacred objects or sites altogether, lest they are potentially impure? Do we leave them an inheritance, and if so, how do we decide how much? Given that the halakhic system is entirely bound to sex/gender, Rabbi Yose's statement leaves us with a rather large conundrum—one which, as Strassfeld says, essentially "exiles the androginos."[35] What does it mean to live outside of a sex/gender system that governs every aspect of life?

Seder Androginos, then, destabilizes the sex/gender binary at the very same moment as it reifies that same binary. As Fausto-Sterling points out, the sages make a bold move that is virtually absent today—introducing a model of biological sex that defies the binary and treating that model as an integral part of their system. However, they are also forever caught in their binary system, unable to shed its remains entirely. The Toseftan text that Fausto-Sterling lauds as "integrating hermaphrodites into mainstream culture" neither expands the binary system to include an *androginos as* an *androginos* nor integrates them as an equal in the sex/gender system.

By creating this "solution" to the "problem" of an *androginos*'s inability to fit their binary categories, the rabbis do not even consider an *androginos* core to that system.

Having laid all of this out, I want to do an about-face for the remainder of this chapter with an attempt at what Eve Kosofsky Sedgwick might term a "reparative reading" of this text.[36] Let me begin with a few caveats. First, I am not suggesting that what I present here is what Rabbi Yose was enacting in his own time and place (though I do like to imagine that he was intersex). Second, I am also not suggesting that I, who am not myself intersex, can (or should) presume to know what might be a liberatory reading of this text for intersex people. I am merely inching my way out onto the thin branch that stretches over any search for integrative or liberatory readings in these texts. I am hopeful that the branch might point toward, or perhaps even serve as a counterpoint to, readings that are proposed when intersex scholars of rabbinics take up these texts in the future. What I have to offer is a familiarity with the texts themselves—a place to start.

The "integration" (I would not call it liberation) that I have found as a non-normate[37] person has come from a mixture of imagination and determination (mine and others'). Here, I put that imagination to work on Rabbi Yose's opinion. Admittedly, what I present here does not *directly* respond to the most pressing undertaking of much intersex activism and scholarship—ending nonconsensual genital surgery—but it does respond *indirectly*. In what follows, I take up a small part of the modern agenda of some intersex activists and scholars—the desire to resist the binary sex/gender system that gives rise to these surgeries to begin with.[38] I do this by thinking about Rabbi Yose through the prism of French philosopher Gilles Deleuze.

How does Deleuze's philosophy comment on this two-thousand-year-old text? In the most famous chapter of his book *Difference and Repetition*, Deleuze presents a two-part argument. He first rejects traditional philosophy's understanding of "thinking," which he derides as circular: "Thought is . . . filled with no more than an image of itself, one in which it recognises itself the more it recognises things."[39] Deleuze then argues for an alternative understanding of thought, in which *difference* can bring about what he calls "encounter": "Something in the world forces us to think. This something is an object not of recognition but of a fundamental encounter. What is encountered may be Socrates, a temple or a demon. It may be grasped in a range of affective tones: wonder, love, hatred, suffering. In whichever tone, its primary characteristic is that it can only be sensed. In this sense it is opposed to recognition."[40]

We must not mistake Deleuze's definition of thought for a simple confrontation with that which "we do not recognize."[41] Rather, he writes, "The conditions of a true critique and a true creation are the same: the destruction of an image of thought which presupposes itself and the genesis of the act of thinking in thought itself."[42] The second characteristic of Deleuze's encounter, therefore, is that the object of that encounter "moves the soul, 'perplexes' it—in other words, *forces it to pose a problem: as though the object of encounter, the sign, were the bearer of a problem—as though it were a problem*" (italics mine).[43]

With these elements in mind, let me return to Seder Androginos to examine it under a Deleuzian microscope. Of course, what the rabbis "know" is a binary sex/gender system. Nowhere in the Torah that they have inherited do we hear of any categories of sex outside of male/female, and their own sex/gender system is, likewise, built on a binary model.[44] We might anticipate "difference," then, in the abyss between their binary sex system and the distinctly nonbinary body of an *androginos*.

In the rabbis' opinion, however, encounter in the Deleuzian sense is absent. Recall that for thinking to occur, the object of the encounter must "force [the soul] to pose a problem." Rather than posing a problem, the rabbis rush to "solve" the potential problem, designing an almost mathematical "fix" that directly calls upon the binary that they already know—precisely the response that Deleuze denounces. The rabbis "remain imprisoned by the same cave or ideas of the times," in Deleuze's words.[45]

Rabbi Yose is another matter. His, I would argue, might be seen as a Deleuzian encounter. What is the object of Rabbi Yose's encounter? Perhaps he, like the other rabbis, is confronted with the conundrum of an *androginos*'s body in contrast with a binary sex/gender system. (I must stress that Deleuze does not consider the "object" of such an encounter the *actual* problem. Rather, he asserts that one encounters the object *as though it were the bearer of a problem*).[46] But perhaps Rabbi Yose's *encounter* is not with *androginoi* at all; perhaps, rather, it is with the rabbis' "solution." After all, how can the rabbis, presumably relaying traditions divinely transmitted, possibly need to shuffle a person back and forth, up and down, just to have them travel through a day? Might the rabbis' response itself stop Rabbi Yose in his tracks?

Regardless of what the "encounter" consists of, Rabbi Yose heads in a different direction. Present-day rabbis and scholars seeking to affirm

queer and nonbinary identities have tended to focus on Rabbi Yose's introduction of what appears to be a third sex/gender option into a binary
matrix.[47] Indeed, that is one way of reading Rabbi Yose's opinion.[48] I
want to argue here, however, that Rabbi Yose himself poses a Deleuzian
"problem" for us, his readers. It is not what he *says* that does so, but
what he *does not say*.[49] In contrast with other rabbinic texts concerning
an *androginos* (which are all halakhic), Rabbi Yose's positioning of an
androginos as a creation sui generis lacks any halakhot. Rabbi Yose offers
no "solution" by which an *androginos* might know how to live under a
halakhic system. He neither excludes and dehumanizes *androginoi* (as
those who later interpret him sometimes do) nor issues directives that
include *androginoi* within the existing framework (as the other rabbis do).
Instead, his encounter is a Deleuzian prod that pulls us out of our own
sex/gender-binary cave—disturbing thought. For Deleuze, an encounter
occurs when the soul is forced to *pose a problem*. Unlike the rabbis, whose
move is to *solve* a problem, indeed, Rabbi Yose *poses* one. How should
an *androginos* perform their gender when they wake up in the morning?
Rabbi Yose is himself stopped short, and therein lies the encounter that
Deleuze seeks—the encounter that sparks genuine thought. So, too, does
Rabbi Yose pass that problem on to us, his readers, who must contend
with his opinion as a problem ourselves—engendering "the new, with its
power of beginning and beginning again."[50]

Of course, reading Rabbi Yose through this prism does not address
the question of the invisibility of intersex people in this text and perhaps
even intensifies the problem. If Rabbi Yose's words are to be understood
as providing a Deleuzian "encounter" by which we may think, if he merely
presents an *androginos* as confounding (even if they are only *perceived* as
such), then Rabbi Yose, in this schema, ignores intersex persons, per se,
altogether. This reading does little, then, to help us, in Strassfeld's words,
"render legible" intersex bodies. Indeed, it is possible that this is not a task
we may expect from these sources, just as we cannot expect the sources
themselves to open a generative space for lesbians or women.[51]

Perhaps, however, we can elicit one step in that direction by building
on the final sentence in intersex scholar Iain Morland's "Postmodern Intersex," written as a response to Alice Dreger: "If the reform project shows
postmodern ethics to be characterized by ambivalence, then I submit
that the ethical way to treat intersexed individuals is to preserve, rather
than to surgically abolish, the uncertainties that their bodies provoke."[52]

I shall leave ambivalent whether Rabbi Yose does what Morland proposes, but let me suggest how we might read Rabbi Yose thus, even if that is not the *only* way to read him. Rabbi Yose appears to leave an *androginos* unmoored—with no instructions for living a halakhic life, that is, with no gender to match their sex. But if we think through Morland's closing statement, it is the majority opinion of the rabbis that seems like the precursor to a system that advocates surgery. Although the rabbis do not consign an *androginos* to a *single* sex/gender, they do consign them to the binary—a system that in our own day culminates in "corrective" surgery.

On the other hand, by denying us a halakhic response, Rabbi Yose does not foreclose the options of what an intersex person's life might look like by delimiting its sex/gender boundaries. Rabbi Yose takes a first step toward forging terrain into which an *androginos* might venture, not as male, female, neither, or both but precisely as sui generis. In Morland's words, Rabbi Yose "preserves the uncertainties" that an *androginos*'s body provokes, allowing that we might allow our Deleuzian encounter with *his* uncertainty to move *us*. Our encounter with Yose drives us to "think" a system in which there is room for an *androginos* to *be* an *androginos*. Perhaps then, in a birthing room of Rabbi Yose's making, we may one day hear the joyous exclamation "it's an intersexual!"

Notes

1. In contemporary parlance, the word can have a far more expansive meaning. See "What Is Intersex?" on the website of the Intersex Society of North America (https://isna.org/faq/what_is_intersex/), which is currently maintained by interACT: Advocates for Intersex Youth. For why I use the modern term *intersex* to describe an ancient category, see Sarra Lev, *And the Sages Did Not Know: Early Rabbinic Approaches to Intersex* (Philadelphia: University of Pennsylvania, forthcoming).

2. See, for example, Emi Koyama, "From 'Intersex' to 'DSD': Toward a Queer Disability Politics of Gender" (keynote, Translating Identity Conference, University of Vermont, Burlington, VT, Intersex Initiative, February 2006), http://www.intersexinitiative.org/articles/intersextodsd.html; Alyson K. Spurgas, "(Un)Queering Identity: The Biosocial Production of Intersex/DSD," in *Critical Intersex*, ed. Morgan Holmes (Burlington, VT: Ashgate Publishing, 2009), 105; Sharon E. Preves, "Out of the O.R. and into the Streets: Exploring the Impact of Intersex

Media Activism," *Research in Political Sociology* 13 (2004), https://doi.org/10.1016/ S0895-9935(04)13006-4. The Androgen Insensitivity Syndrome Support Group (AISSG) website posted a severe statement, which has since been removed. The original statement can be accessed at "What Is AIS?," last updated September 13, 2006, https://web.archive.org/web/20070627172426/https://www.aissg.org/21_ OVERVIEW.HTM. It is also quoted in Spurgas, "(Un)Queering Identity," 106. See also Hil Malatino, *Queer Embodiment: Monstrosity, Medical Violence, and Intersex Experience* (Lincoln: University of Nebraska Press, 2019), 78. Malatino does not object outright but calls on feminists to keep intersex issues front and center when doing this work.

3. See, for example, Susannah Temko, "A Different Kind of Superpower: What It Means to Be Intersex," presented at TEDxLondon 2019, https://tedxlondon.com/topic/society/a-different-kind-of-superpower-what-it-means-to-be-intersex-susannah-temko-tedxlondon/; Anunnaki Ray Marquez, "Born Intersex: We Are Human!," presented at TEDxJacksonville 2018; Meghan McDonough, "How Medicine's Fixation on the Sex Binary Harms Intersex People," *A Question of Sex*, episode 2, Scientific American documentary, August 24, 2022, https:// www.scientificamerican.com/article/how-medicines-fixation-on-the-sex-binary-harms-intersex-people1/. I should note also that this chapter is a small slice of a much larger project in which I explore the early rabbinic landscape as a whole and its (hypothetical) implications for intersex persons living under rabbinic halakhah (Lev, *Sages*).

4. The history I speak of is a history of discourse rather than a history of people. Unfortunately, the latter is unattainable within the context of rabbinic literature.

5. Morgan Holmes, "Queer Cut Bodies," in *Queer Frontiers: Millennial Geographies, Genders, and Generations*, ed. Joseph A. Boone et al. (Madison: University of Wisconsin Press, 2000), 94.

6. Holmes, "Queer Cut Bodies," 89, quoting Anne Fausto-Sterling, "How Many Sexes Are There?," op-ed, *New York Times*, March 12, 1993.

7. Holmes, "Queer Cut Bodies," 89.

8. Holmes, 99.

9. Holmes, 100.

10. Anne Fausto-Sterling, "The Five Sexes: Why Male and Female Are Not Enough," *Sciences* 33, no. 2 (March/April 1993): 20–21, https://doi.org/10.1002/ j.2326-1951.1993.tb03081.x.

11. Anne Fausto-Sterling, *Sexing the Body: Gender Politics and the Construction of Sexuality* (New York: Basic Books, 2000), 31.

12. The rabbis view an *androginos* as having male *and* female genitals. The other category of intersex in rabbinic literature is the *tumtum*, a person with male *or* female genitals but whose genitals are "concealed" and therefore undiscernible.

13. A title coined by Charlotte Fonrobert, who has written several papers on the subject. See Charlotte Elisheva Fonrobert, "Gender Duality and Its Subversions

in Rabbinic Law," in *Gender in Judaism and Islam: Common Lives, Uncommon Heritage*, ed. Firoozeh Kashani-Sabet and Beth S. Wenger (New York: New York University Press, 2015), 115–16. This chapter is informed by the work of both Fonrobert and Max Strassfeld, who reads this text in Max Strassfeld, "Translating the Human: The *Androginos* in Tosefta Bikurim," *Transgender Studies Quarterly* 3, no. 3–4 (2016), and Max K. Strassfeld, *Trans Talmud: Androgynes and Eunuchs in Rabbinic Literature* (Oakland: University of California Press, 2022). See also Charlotte Elisheva Fonrobert, "The Semiotics of the Sexed Body in Early Halakhic Discourse," in *How Should Rabbinic Literature Be Read in the Modern World?*, ed. Matthew Kraus (Piscataway, NJ: Gorgias Press, 2006); Charlotte Elisheva Fonrobert, "Regulating the Human Body: Rabbinic Legal Discourse and the Making of Jewish Gender," in *The Cambridge Companion to the Talmud and Rabbinic Literature*, ed. Charlotte Elisheva Fonrobert and Martin S. Jaffee (Cambridge: Cambridge University Press, 2007).

14. Literally, "[legally] equal to."

15. I use the Vienna manuscript of Tosefta Bikkurim 2:3–7 as my primary text in this chapter. Some manuscripts of the Mishnah also contain a version of this Toseftan text, and there is some debate over which version is primary. While there are several variations between manuscripts even in the Tosefta, the text remains relatively consistent. All translations are mine unless otherwise indicated.

16. Catherine Hezser, "The Graeco-Roman Context of Jewish Daily Life in Roman Palestine," in *The Oxford Handbook of Jewish Daily Life in Roman Palestine*, ed. Catherine Hezser (New York: Oxford University Press, 2010).

17. Exposure entailed being left somewhere to die. If someone came across the child before they died, the child was sometimes enslaved. See W. V. Harris, "Child-Exposure in the Roman Empire," *Journal of Roman Studies* 84 (1994), https://doi.org/10.2307/300867; Lin Foxhall, *Studying Gender in Classical Antiquity* (New York: Cambridge University Press, 2013), 52; Luc Brisson, *Sexual Ambivalence: Androgyny and Hermaphroditism in Graeco-Roman Antiquity* (Berkeley: University of California Press, 2002); Sandra R. Joshel and Sheila Murnaghan, *Women and Slaves in Greco-Roman Culture: Differential Equations* (London: Routledge, 1998), 243, 255–56.

18. Marie Delcourt, *Hermaphrodite: Myths and Rites of the Bisexual Figure in Classical Antiquity* (London: Studio Books, 1961), 45; A. B. Gough, *Appendices and Notes (from the Sixth Edition)*, vol. 4 of *Roman Life and Manners under the Early Empire*, by Ludwig Friedländer (London: George Routledge & Sons, 1913), 4.

19. For an extensive discussion of the figure of the *androginos* in Greek and Roman antiquity, see Brisson, *Sexual Ambivalence*.

20. Dig. 1.5.10. Alan Watson, ed., *The Digest of Justinian*, rev. English language ed. (Philadelphia: University of Pennsylvania Press, 1998), vol. 1. Justinian's Digest is a collection of laws compiled by the emperor Justinian.

21. A similar list exists for the *koy*, a category I discuss below, in Mishnah Bikkurim 2:8–11.

22. Fausto-Sterling, *Sexing the Body*, 33.

23. Jacob Neusner, *Judaism: The Evidence of the Mishnah* (Chicago: University of Chicago Press, 1981), 238.

24. Their discussion is, however, much less developed in the Tosefta than in some manuscripts of the Mishnah.

25. For more on the *koy* and hybridity, see Strassfeld, *Trans Talmud*, 66–72.

26. See Fonrobert, "Regulating," 287. That the figure of an *androginos* appears quite regularly in contemporaneous Roman sources, including in Roman law, lends credibility to the position that the rabbinic discussion was not merely a theoretical one; so, too, do current statistics marking the relative commonality of intersex births. Although it is anachronistic to apply current statistics to the ancient world, there is no reason to assume that such births did not occur at least as regularly as they do now. See A. Rösler, A. Bélanger, and F. Labrie, "Mechanisms of Androgen Production in Male Pseudohermaphroditism due to 17 Beta-Hydroxysteroid Dehydrogenase Deficiency," *Journal of Clinical Endocrinology & Metabolism* 75, no. 3 (September 1992), https://doi.org/10.1210/jcem.75.3.1325474; Julianne Imperato-McGinley et al., "Steroid 5α-Reductase Deficiency in Man: An Inherited Form of Male Pseudohermaphroditism," *Science* 186, no. 4170 (December 27, 1974); Sharon E. Sytsma, ed., *Ethics and Intersex* (Dordrecht, the Netherlands: Springer, 2006). Regarding projecting today's statistics back to late antiquity, see also Veronique Dasen, "Multiple Births in Graeco-Roman Antiquity," *Oxford Journal of Archaeology* 16, no. 1 (1997): 58, https://doi.org/10.1111/1468-0092.00024.

27. Named opinions in early rabbinic sources are generally understood by the later sources as minority opinions and, usually, as disagreeing with the anonymous majority.

28. See the previous note.

29. There are exceptions to this principle. See Lev, *Sages*, chapter 6.

30. Chapter 12 of Leviticus declares a woman who gave birth "impure," for lack of a better translation. The notion of impurity in scripture is complex, but for our purposes here, genital emissions by both men and women are sources of "impurity." Following a period of impurity, the impure person must dedicate a sacrifice to the temple.

31. Although, as Iain Morland similarly points out of culture today, "personhood in Western culture is not defined as being half male half female. Concomitantly, personhood places a prohibition upon beings that really are half male half female." Iain Morland, "Is Intersexuality Real?," *Textual Practice* 15, no. 3 (2001): 533–34. For the thin line between human and other-than-human in Palestinian rabbinic literature, see Rachel Rafael Neis, "Fetus, Flesh, Food: Generating Bodies of Knowledge in Rabbinic Science," *Journal of Ancient Judaism* 10, no. 2 (2019); Rachel Neis, "The Reproduction of Species: Humans, Animals and Species Nonconformity in Early Rabbinic Science," *Jewish Studies Quarterly* 24, no. 4 (2017), https://doi.org/10.1628/094457017X15072727130648; and Rafael Neis,

"Interspecies and Cross-Species Generation: Limits and Potentialities in Tannaitic Reproductive Science," in *Strength to Strength: Essays in Appreciation of Shaye J. D. Cohen*, ed. Michael L. Satlow (Providence, RI: Brown Judaic Studies, 2018). For an exploration of the category *human* in Avodah Zarah, see Mira Wasserman, *Jews, Gentiles, and Other Animals: The Talmud after the Humanities* (Philadelphia: University of Pennsylvania Press, 2017).

32. Strassfeld, "Translating," 596.

33. Tosefta Bikkurim, 2:7.

34. Strassfeld, *Trans Talmud*, 80–81.

35. Strassfeld, "Translating," 597.

36. Eve Kosofsky Sedgwick, *Touching Feeling: Affect, Pedagogy, Performativity* (Durham, NC: Duke University Press, 2003), chapter 4. This reading does not negate my previous assertions or Strassfeld's compelling lens of exile but instead offers a counterpoint while always keeping in mind the alternative.

37. The term *normate* was coined by Rosemarie Garland-Thomson in her book on disability, *Extraordinary Bodies*. As Garland-Thomson explains, the term refers to "the constructed identity of those who, by way of the bodily configurations and cultural capital they assume, can step into a position of authority and wield the power it grants them." Rosemarie Garland-Thomson, *Extraordinary Bodies: Figuring Physical Disability in American Culture and Literature* (New York: Columbia University Press, 1997), 8.

38. See, for example, Holmes, "Queer Cut Bodies," 89.

39. Deleuze's words here comment on a statement by Socrates in Plato's *Republic*. See Plato, *Republic* 7.523a–524a. Gilles Deleuze, *Difference and Repetition*, trans. Paul Patton (New York: Columbia University Press, 1994), 138.

40. Deleuze, *Difference*, 140.

41. Deleuze, 138–39.

42. Deleuze, 139.

43. Deleuze, 140.

44. See Fonrobert, "Gender Duality," especially 109–10. See also Fonrobert, "Semiotics," on the Roman sex/gender system in which the rabbis were situated, which incorporated intersex bodies.

45. Deleuze, *Difference*, 134.

46. Note the essential point in Deleuze's view, that an *androginos* themself does not constitute a problem but only *appears* to the person in the encounter as a problem. There is nothing about an intersex body that is inherently perplexing. Rather, in a system of binary sex/gender, whoever lies outside that binary is "perplexing" in the Deleuzian sense. See also Gregory Flaxman, *Gilles Deleuze and the Fabulation of Philosophy* (Minneapolis: University of Minnesota Press, 2012), 182.

47. See, for example, Elliot Kukla, "A Created Being of Its Own: Toward a Jewish Liberation Theology for Men, Women and Everyone Else," *TransTorah*, 2006, http://transtorah.org/PDFs/How_I_Met_the_Tumtum.pdf; Gwynn Kessler,

"Rabbinic Gender: Beyond Male and Female," in *A Companion to Late Ancient Jews and Judaism: Third Century BCE to Seventh Century CE*, ed. Naomi Koltun-Fromm and Gwynn Kessler (Hoboken, NJ: Wiley, 2020).

48. For other opinions, see Strassfeld, *Trans Talmud*, 79–80; Lev, *Sages*, chapter 3.

49. I also shift away from thinking about nonbinary identity and toward thinking about intersex in particular. Why? When I came out in the 1980s, lesbian needs were often subordinated to the agendas of gay men in the gay liberation movement and straight women in the women's movement. While I am a nonbinary lesbian, and while everything I say in this chapter could support nonbinary and queer identities, I am wary of displacing the agendas of intersex people as mine were displaced long ago.

50. Deleuze, *Difference*, 136.

51. A tip of the keyboard to Mel Bramyn, who used to call out "Lesbians and women!" when making an announcement at the Midwest Lesbian Festival.

52. Iain Morland, "Postmodern Intersex," in Sytsma, *Ethics and Intersex*, 331. Morland's chapter responds to the epilogue in Alice D. Dreger, *Hermaphrodites and the Medical Invention of Sex* (Cambridge, MA: Harvard University Press, 1998).

References

Brisson, Luc. *Sexual Ambivalence Androgyny and Hermaphroditism in Graeco-Roman Antiquity*. Joan Palevsky Imprint in Classical Literature. Berkeley: University of California Press, 2002.

Dasen, Veronique. "Multiple Births in Graeco-Roman Antiquity." *Oxford Journal of Archaeology* 16, no. 1 (1997): 49–63. https://doi.org/10.1111/1468-0092.00024.

Delcourt, Marie. *Hermaphrodite; Myths and Rites of the Bisexual Figure in Classical Antiquity*. London: Studio Books, 1961.

Deleuze, Gilles. *Difference and Repetition*. Translated by Paul Patton. New York: Columbia University Press, 1994.

Dreger, Alice D. *Hermaphrodites and the Medical Invention of Sex*. Cambridge, MA: Harvard University Press, 1998.

Fausto-Sterling, Anne. *Sexing the Body: Gender Politics and the Construction of Sexuality*. New York: Basic Books, 2000.

Flaxman, Gregory. *Gilles Deleuze and the Fabulation of Philosophy*. Minneapolis: University of Minnesota Press, 2012.

Fonrobert, Charlotte Elisheva. "Gender Duality and Its Subversions in Rabbinic Law." In *Gender in Judaism and Islam: Common Lives, Uncommon Heritage*, edited by Firoozeh Kashani-Sabet and Beth S. Wenger, 106–25. New York: New York University Press, 2015.

———. "Regulating the Human Body: Rabbinic Legal Discourse and the Making of Jewish Gender." In *The Cambridge Companion to the Talmud and Rabbinic Literature*, edited by Charlotte Elisheva Fonrobert and Martin S. Jaffee, 270–94. Cambridge Companions to Religion. Cambridge: Cambridge University Press, 2007.

———. "The Semiotics of the Sexed Body in Early Halakhic Discourse." In *How Should Rabbinic Literature Be Read in the Modern World?*, edited by Matthew Kraus, 79–105. Judaism in Context. Piscataway, NJ: Gorgias Press, 2006.

Foxhall, Lin. *Studying Gender in Classical Antiquity: Key Themes in Ancient History.* New York: Cambridge University Press, 2013.

Garland-Thomson, Rosemarie. *Extraordinary Bodies: Figuring Physical Disability in American Culture and Literature.* New York: Columbia University Press, 1997.

Gough, A. G. *Appendices and Notes (from the Sixth Edition).* Vol. 4 of *Roman Life and Manners under the Early Empire*, by Ludwig Friedländer. London: George Routledge & Sons, 1913.

Harris, W. V. "Child-Exposure in the Roman Empire." *Journal of Roman Studies* 84 (1994): 1–22. https://doi.org/10.2307/300867.

Hezser, Catherine. "The Graeco-Roman Context of Jewish Daily Life in Roman Palestine." In *The Oxford Handbook of Jewish Daily Life in Roman Palestine*, edited by Catherine Hezser, 28–47. Oxford Handbooks in Classics and Ancient History. New York: Oxford University Press, 2010.

Holmes, Morgan. "Queer Cut Bodies." In *Queer Frontiers: Millennial Geographies, Genders, and Generations*, edited by Joseph A. Boone, Martin Dupuis, Martin Meeker, Karin Quimby, Cindy Sarver, Debra Silverman, and Rosemary Weatherston, 84–110. Madison: University of Wisconsin Press, 1999.

Imperato-McGinley, Julianne, Luis Guerrero, Teofilo Gautier, and Ralph E. Peterson. "Steroid 5α-Reductase Deficiency in Man: An Inherited Form of Male Pseudohermaphroditism." *Science* 186, no. 4170 (December 27, 1974): 1213–15.

Joshel, Sandra R., and Sheila Murnaghan. *Women and Slaves in Greco-Roman Culture: Differential Equations.* London: Routledge, 1998.

Kessler, Gwynn. "Rabbinic Gender: Beyond Male and Female." In *A Companion to Late Ancient Jews and Judaism: Third Century BCE to Seventh Century CE*, edited by Naomi Koltun-Fromm and Gwynn Kessler, 353–70. Hoboken, NJ: Wiley, 2020.

Koyama, Emi. "From 'Intersex' to 'DSD': Toward a Queer Disability Politics of Gender." Keynote at the Translating Identity Conference, University of Vermont, Burlington, VT, February 2006. http://www.intersexinitiative.org/articles/intersextodsd.html.

Lev, Sarra. *And the Sages Did Not Know: Intersex in Early Rabbinic Literature.* Philadelphia: University of Pennsylvania, forthcoming.

Malatino, Hil. *Queer Embodiment: Monstrosity, Medical Violence, and Intersex Experience*. Lincoln: University of Nebraska Press, 2019.

Morland, Iain. "Is Intersexuality Real?" *Textual Practice* 15, no. 3 (2001): 527–47.

———. "Postmodern Intersex." In Sytsma, *Ethics and Intersex*, 319–32.

Neis, Rachel Rafael. "Fetus, Flesh, Food: Generating Bodies of Knowledge in Rabbinic Science." *Journal of Ancient Judaism* 10, no. 2 (2019): 181–210.

———. "Interspecies and Cross-species Generation: Limits and Potentialities in Tannaitic Reproductive Science." In *Strength to Strength: Essays in Appreciation of Shaye J. D. Cohen*, edited by Michael L. Satlow, 309–28. Providence, RI: Brown Judaic Studies, 2018.

———. "The Reproduction of Species: Humans, Animals and Species Nonconformity in Early Rabbinic Science." *Jewish Studies Quarterly* 24, no. 4 (2017): 289–317. https://doi.org/10.1628/094457017X15072727130648.

Neusner, Jacob. *Judaism: The Evidence of the Mishnah*. Chicago: University of Chicago Press, 1981.

Preves, Sharon E. "Out of the O.R. and into the Streets: Exploring the Impact of Intersex Media Activism." *Research in Political Sociology* 13 (2004): 179–223. https://doi.org/10.1016/S0895-9935(04)13006-4.

Rösler, A., A. Bélanger, and F. Labrie. "Mechanisms of Androgen Production in Male Pseudohermaphroditism due to 17 Beta-Hydroxysteroid Dehydrogenase Deficiency." *Journal of Clinical Endocrinology & Metabolism* 75, no. 3 (September 1992): 773–78. https://doi.org/10.1210/jcem.75.3.1325474.

Sedgwick, Eve Kosofsky. *Touching Feeling: Affect, Pedagogy, Performativity*. Durham, NC: Duke University Press, 2003.

Spurgas, Alyson K. "(Un)Queering Identity: The Biosocial Production of Intersex/DSD." In *Critical Intersex*, edited by Morgan Holmes, 97–122. Burlington, VT: Ashgate Publishing, 2009.

Strassfeld, Max. "Translating the Human: The Androginos in Tosefta Bikurim." *Transgender Studies Quarterly* 3, no. 3–4 (2016): 587–604.

———. *Trans Talmud: Androgynes and Eunuchs in Rabbinic Literature*. Oakland: University of California Press, 2022.

Sytsma, Sharon E., editor. *Ethics and Intersex*. International Library of Ethics, Law, and the New Medicine, vol. 29. Dordrecht, the Netherlands: Springer, 2006.

Wasserman, Mira. *Jews, Gentiles, and Other Animals: The Talmud after the Humanities*. Philadelphia: University of Pennsylvania Press, 2017.

Watson, Alan, editor. *The Digest of Justinian*. Rev. English language ed. Philadelphia: University of Pennsylvania Press, 1998. 2 vols.

Chapter 3

At the Intersection of Sephardic, Mizrahi, and LGBTQ+

The Story of a Community Emerging out of the Margins

Ruben Shimonov and Marielle Tawil

The *hamsa*[1] is an ancient palm-shaped amulet that has been used for protection by communities throughout North Africa, West Asia/the Middle East,[2] and the Mediterranean. According to folk tradition, the *hamsa* wards off evil energy and brings its owners blessings and good fortune. It often contains within it another ancient motif that communicates safeguarding: a stylized eye. This symbol of safety serves as the logo of the Sephardic Mizrahi Q Network (SMQN), a grassroots movement that works to build an enriching and supportive community for an often-overlooked segment of the Jewish world: LGBTQ+ Sephardic and Mizrahi Jews.[3] SMQN's *hamsa*, however, has a few unique particularities. It is filled in with a rainbow color scheme, which conveys the organization's mission to create a safe and welcoming space for its LGBTQ+ members.[4] Adorning the logo are the protective Jewish symbols of the Magen David (Shield of David) and an illuminated menorah, as well as arabesque floral patterns and a mosaic that signifies both the diversity and togetherness of SMQN's eclectic community.

Since its inception in 2016, those engaged with the Sephardic Mizrahi Q Network have been committed to creating an empowering and nurturing platform for the intersection of LGBTQ+ and Sephardic-Mizrahi life—a platform that uplifts and celebrates the multilayered identities of queer Mizrahi and Sephardic Jews. From the first days creating our movement, we felt propelled by a sense of urgency—an understanding that there needed to be a vibrant space where LGBTQ+ Sephardic and Mizrahi Jews could proudly bring their full selves without checking any part of their complex identities at the door. Two essential questions drove our initial endeavors: (1) Where do we, as queer Sephardic and Mizrahi Jews in the United States, fully belong? (2) Are there any spaces in which we can show up as our complete and authentic selves without needing to leave behind or minimize any part of who we are?

The sobering reality was that such an environment did not exist. Existing organized LGBTQ+ Jewish spaces did not fully resonate with many of us, as they lacked Sephardic and Mizrahi membership and representation in leadership as well as regular programming that speaks to our intersectional identities. A relatively recent term that has emerged to explain this phenomenon is *Ashkenormativity*, "the systemic, communal, and/or individual assertion of Ashkenazi as the default Jewish identity, the assumptions we make based on that assertion, and the resulting marginalization of non-Ashkenazi Jews" in both Jewish and non-Jewish spaces.[5] As the scholars Analucia Lopezrevoredo and David Schraub point out, "in general, American Jewish organizations right, left, and center are notorious for being Ashkenormative—in other words, making the Ashkenazi experience the de-facto Jewish experience."[6] Ashkenormativity ultimately harms us all, not just Sephardic and Mizrahi Jews, as it denies everyone—Jews and non-Jews alike—the opportunity to appreciate the true diversity and multifaceted nature of the Jewish people.[7]

Yet Ashkenormativity tells but one part of the tale, albeit an important one. In our own Mizrahi and Sephardic communities, while many of us have felt a deep connection to the richness of our traditions, heritage, and history, we have found it difficult to feel a complete sense of belonging because of anti-LGBTQ+ sentiments. Homophobia and transphobia in traditional communities are complex and nonmonolithic issues that cannot be painted with a broad stroke. Indeed, it would be too simplistic, and deeply problematic, to assume that "traditional Middle Eastern values" are the culprit. Nevertheless, due to a combination of multiple factors—including immigration, historical trauma, minority status, and family norms—many LGBTQ+ Sephardic and Mizrahi Jews have felt varying degrees of alienation from their family's communities, even as they feel a profound attachment to their deep-rooted cultures. In summary, many of us at the intersection of being queer and Sephardic-Mizrahi find ourselves constantly compartmentalizing various parts of our identities, hardly able to show up as our full selves. Being in such a liminal space, in which one feels neither here nor there, is both painful and exhausting.

To begin addressing this critical gap, we started building a virtual community on social media. Our private Facebook group became a vibrant digital space for LGBTQ+ Sephardic and Mizrahi Jews to connect, communicate, and feel like they belong. For many, the group was deeply affirming, showing them that they are not alone in their struggle. As one member described, "It was an incredible discovery—exactly what I needed! A place to be Bukharian, to be Mizrahi, and to be queer. . . . I didn't leave anything behind. Not my queerness, not my gender, not my religion, and not my culture." Our network organically grew as existing members added more individuals to the online community. Over time, a strong interest emerged in meeting in person. When thinking about how we might want to gather outside of the digital realm, it seemed most compelling to come together over a Shabbat meal. For many Sephardic and Mizrahi Jews, a connection to Shabbat runs very deep. In our families' homes, the aromas, melodies, tastes, languages, and spirit of our heritage would be present at the Shabbat table. We wanted to recreate that atmosphere but also enhance it by building a queer-affirming space—a space in which one's LGBTQ+ and Sephardic-Mizrahi identities did not have to be in tension with one another. In February 2017, we hosted our first Friday-night dinner and thus began the tradition of our monthly pop-up Shabbat dinners, which have now happened in the homes of dozens of our community members in the greater New York City area.

These dinners have become a cornerstone of our movement, anchoring our community in something simultaneously ancient and innovative. The dinners create a warm and inviting space for individuals to develop friendships, establish support systems, and bring—for the very first time, for some—their entire selves to the Shabbat experience. Over Syrian kibbeh (deep-fried cracked bulgur wheat stuffed with flavorful chopped meat), Persian *ghormeh sabzi* (a savory and sour Iranian herb stew), spicy Moroccan fish, or numerous other North African and West Asian dishes, people come together for a dynamic Shabbat experience in which they can feel fully seen and heard. As one person, who has since become a board member, expressed, "I am so grateful for the Sephardic Mizrahi Q Network. When I was first coming to terms with my queer identity,

I stumbled across their Shabbat dinners online. I could not believe that there was a community group specifically for queer Sephardic and Mizrahi Jews—specifically catered to my identity. It felt like a lifeline. To this day, it still does. I have never felt more seen, more loved, and more accepted by any group." Another community member explained, "As a first-generation Iranian Jewish lesbian, community has always been a vital element in my life—however, usually separated. The SMQN LGBTQ+ Shabbat dinners build a community where, with others, I'm now able to weave all facets of my identity together, build friendships, and feel at peace through our shared traditions and stories." For some, the dinners are a time to connect with old friends and meet new ones. For others, it goes a step further: it is a reliable gathering and is the only time they can bring their full selves to a Jewish space—and have that celebrated. "I showed up at my first SMQN dinner and found home," a Syrian Jewish member expressed. "I met some of my best friends that night. The monthly Shabbat dinners are truly a time that I look forward to. It's a safe, warm and supportive space that I'm guaranteed at least once a month. It's a time to unwind and be my true self, surrounded by people who see me and all of my intersecting identities. I feel as though I found safety, comfort and friendship with my SMQN family."

The concept of a chosen family is a crucial part of the LGBTQ+ experience. It is connected to a deep desire of individuals who have endured struggle to feel at home. "SMQN is family, community and love. The support of this community has allowed me to live my life with pride and confidence, which in turn has strengthened and fused my Jewish and LGBTQ identity," said a Persian Jewish member. An Iraqi Israeli echoed this sentiment when she wrote, "SMQN is my second family. While I am involved in other queer Jewish groups in NYC, SMQN is the only thing of its kind—by and for Sephardic/Mizrahi queers. There is no need to check any part of your identity at the door. It's nice being able to access Jewish culture without expectation of a certain level of observance." Similarly, another member shared, "I was a minority as a gay man in a Mizrahi community, and again as a Mizrahi man in a very accepting progressive Jewish American community. SMQN is where I was able to blend both aspects of these identities and finally feel at home."

Our dinners have created an opportunity for different folks to take on leadership roles as they host or help plan each gathering. In doing so, individuals are able to reconnect to, and reclaim, their family's traditions in ways that are meaningful to them. This collaborative leadership and community-building model—which inspires members to take ownership of their Jewish journeys on their own terms and to play an active role in creating the community they want to see—has informed all of our programming. As we have grown, so have the different ways in which we gather and build our community. A year into hosting our monthly home-based Shabbat dinners, we started gathering in nonapartment venues once a season due to the growing demand of the dinners. Beyond Friday night, we have hosted regular Shabbat lunches, Havdalah gatherings, *shabbaton* retreats, egalitarian Shabbat services, learning programs, and discussion groups. For the latter, we have piloted initiatives such as the Arts + Culture Café and SMQN Beit Midrash—spaces for creative expression, in-depth learning about Sephardic and Mizrahi histories, and discussions on various topics relevant to LGBTQ+ and Sephardic-Mizrahi life. All of these community-driven programs have become opportunities for our members to feel empowered as leaders and co-creators of our eclectic community. The collaborative nature of SMQN encourages our members to contribute to the continuous building and strengthening of our movement.

Our community has intentionally been a traveling one, showing up in the homes of our members. We have also gathered in different Jewish centers that support our endeavors. Such places include the Jewish Community Center of Harlem (JCC Harlem), which has become a strong partner in our work. The institutional support that we have received is a beautiful indication of the ways in which the needle of diversity is being moved forward in the US Jewish world. In building our community, the Sephardic Mizrahi Q Network relied on the tangible experience of gathering in person in a physical community with people, foods, arts, and cultures.

With the spread of the COVID-19 global pandemic, SMQN needed to pivot and adapt our programming to virtual spaces for the safety of our members. More than even before, it is imperative for SMQN to be a resource and support system for our community. While the shift to virtual gatherings has brought a new set of challenges, the virtual gatherings have also allowed us to engage members of our community that live outside of New York City, in places across the US and around the world. In thinking about how we could creatively adapt to the precarious times and continue to be a much-needed hub for our community, we launched new programs such as "Chai and Chat," a series of dynamic conversations with different members of SMQN's diverse community. At each virtual program, a community member talks about their professional work, community leadership, and personal Jewish and LGBTQ+ journeys.

Over the course of about four years, SMQN has hosted more than one hundred gatherings that have engaged a community of nearly eight hundred members. In filling a critical communal gap, we are not only creating a necessary hub for a community that has been relegated to the margins but also enriching the broader Jewish and LGBTQ+ worlds. As one of our members explained, SMQN's "existence is so important—not just for queer Jews going through their own individual journeys but collectively as a group to show the greater Jewish, Sephardic, [and] LGBTQ+ world that Jews of all backgrounds, orientations, and genders exist." Elevating the experiences of LGBTQ+ Sephardic and Mizrahi Jews enriches everyone by adding to the rich mosaic of the Jewish people. Therefore, while rooted in a commitment to lifting up the voices of Sephardic and Mizrahi queer folks, our community welcomes all LGBTQ+ individuals who want to connect to our mission. Our community brings together LGBTQ+ Jews from a multitude of Sephardic and Mizrahi backgrounds and beyond. We welcome anyone who wants to share in celebrating the rich, multilayered experiences of LGBTQ+ Mizrahi and Sephardic Jews. Furthermore, while the majority of our programming directly supports LGBTQ+ folks, we understand the importance of engaging allies and building partnerships with stakeholders in the broader Sephardic, Mizrahi, and Jewish worlds. We envision a world in which the diverse stories and experiences of LGBTQ+ Mizrahi and Sephardic Jews are better understood and embraced by LGBTQ+ organizations, both in the Jewish world and beyond, as well as by Sephardic and Mizrahi communities and institutions. Thus, we also host more public-facing programming, such as educational seminars on diversity and inclusivity; support opportunities for Sephardic and Mizrahi family members of LGBTQ+ individuals; and create collaborative programs together with other organizations, such as the JCC Harlem, American Sephardi Federation, Moishe House, and UJA-Federation of New York. These partnerships demonstrate that the broader Jewish world is recognizing our community as an essential part of the Jewish collective.

At the heart of SMQN's community is an understanding that no one should have to forgo or sacrifice any part of their identity for another. Many of our members have expressed the significance of this in their lives. "Before SMQN," one of them wrote, "I thought pursuing my life as an out gay man meant that I had to leave behind my Syrian Jewish identity because there were no spaces out there for Mizrahi Queer Jews like myself, especially in areas related to religious customs and prayer. I remember attending a Friday night egalitarian service hosted at a member's house. That was the night it hit me that I didn't have to leave that part of my identity behind. That is what SMQN did for me and continues to do for others." Similarly, another member said, "Being a part of the SMQN has meant so much to my partner and me. I never could have imagined a place where my identities as a queer, Jewish, and Sephardic woman could come together with such ease. My partner and I often say how grateful we are to experience the warmth of Shabbat while showing up as our whole authentic selves. . . . It's truly a blessing in our lives." Essential to our community-building work is the commitment to raising up one another's diverse voices and life experiences so that we all feel seen, heard, and supported. In doing this work, the *hamsa* of the Sephardic Mizrahi Q Network shines brighter and more luminously with each day, bringing greater protection, safety, and joy to its eclectic community.

Notes

1. A more accurate transliteration of the Arabic word خمسة is *khamsa*, but this chapter will employ the most frequently used English transliteration, which is *hamsa*.

2. While the term *Middle East* is more commonly used to describe this region, it is problematic due to its Eurocentric and colonial history. This chapter will refer to the region as *West Asia*. We acknowledge, however, that even the latter term does not have clearly defined borders because of the varying ways in which global regions are delimited in social and political discourse.

3. As with all identity terms, *Sephardic* and *Mizrahi* are socially constructed and fluid; thus they carry meanings that vary with time, place, and community. For our purposes, we use both words together to refer to Jewish communities with deep roots in the Iberian Peninsula, North Africa, West Asia/the Middle East, the Balkans, Central Asia, and the Caucasus. As with other umbrella terms, *Mizrahi* and *Sephardic* run the risk of painting with a broad stroke the cultures and experiences of different communities. Yet these terms also have the power to highlight stories and experiences on the margins, as well as to transcend differences among cultural elements.

4. *LGBTQ+* is an acronym for lesbian, gay, bisexual, transgender, and queer or questioning. These terms are used to describe a person's sexual orientation and/or gender identity. The addition of + is used to encompass spectra

of sexuality and gender. As an umbrella term for sexual- and gender-minority communities who are not heterosexual or are not cisgender, the word *queer* will be used interchangeably with *LGBTQ+* in this chapter.

5. Jay M. Stanton, "Ashkenormativity Is Twice as Common—and Harmful—in LGBTQ Jewish Spaces," op-ed, *Forward*, August 24, 2015, https://forward.com/opinion/319640/why-ashkenormativity-is-twice-as-common-and-harmful-in-lgbtq-jewish-spaces/.

6. Analucia Lopezrevoredo and David Schraub, "An Intersectional Failure: How Both Israel's Backers and Critics Write Mizrahi Jews Out of the Story," *Tablet*, January 25, 2016, https://www.tabletmag.com/scroll/197169/an-intersectional-failure-how-both-israels-backers-and-critics-write-mizrahi-jews-out-of-the-story.

7. In recent years, heightened awareness of this pressing issue in the American Jewish world has led many Jewish organizations to begin to engage with this institutional problem. We applaud the progress while also recognizing that there is still much room for growth.

Chapter 4

ID, Please

VINNY CALVO PRELL

The first thing I learned about lesbianism is that a lesbian is a woman who loves other women—romantically, sexually, or otherwise.

The second thing I learned about lesbianism is that the best kind of lesbian to be is a Gold Star lesbian—one who has never kissed, fondled, or fucked a man.

(Next up was my realization that I was definitely not a lesbian.)

I've learned a lot of things about lesbianism, but those two lessons have always stuck with me. I always felt like there was a possibility—if you were a lesbian—that another lesbian could revoke your membership. Like that sickening and unpredictable feeling of falling that sometimes happens as one falls asleep, there was always the creeping possibility that the safety and protection of the lesbian community could all fall away in an instant. Any disagreement with the majority of lesbians was dangerous. It was simply better off to like the same lesbian music, join the lesbian protest at the march, and eat at the local lesbian hangout (assuming, of course, there was enough of a lesbian community to sustain these where you lived). This precariousness, of course, is hardly limited to the lesbian community.

Over decades of involvement in the women's movement, I've watched organizations fall apart during arguments about who belonged and who was an interloper.

Without a doubt, the most unexpected moment of free fall I experienced was during a conversation with a dear friend and mentor. I was talking about my childhood experiences with Judaism, and I mentioned that my mom isn't ritually Jewish. She raised Jewish children but never converted to Judaism. In response to this footnote, my friend suggested that it would be better for me not to chant Torah in our congregation in the future. His comment was so unexpected that I was almost unable to respond. Why shouldn't I chant Torah? What could possibly be the problem? The reason was clear to him: because I lacked a Jewish mother and a ritual conversion, some members of our congregation wouldn't consider me Jewish. At his words, the ground fell away beneath me. I wasn't Jewish? My parents named me in my temple at eight days old. I attended religious school, became a bat mitzvah, worked as an assistant teacher in the religious school, became confirmed, served on my temple youth group board, attended Jewish summer camp, led services at my college Hillel, and served on our synagogue's board. And yet, somehow, I wasn't Jewish.

That conversation took place fifteen years ago. He never mentioned it again, leaving me to wonder why it was so important to share in the first place. Who were the unnamed members of the congregation whose possible objections mattered more than my actual Jewish practice? How could someone who knew me so intimately dismiss my Judaism? It was not the first time someone questioned my Judaism, and it certainly won't be the last. As a Jewish professional, I've ended up in a number of conversations about how "of course Jews from interfaith and mixed-race families don't affiliate," and every time it's as though a stranger passing on the sidewalk has shoved me. It feels as though I'm that little kid in school, frantically waving my hand to answer the question, and the teacher's eyes are skipping over me, seeking someone else to please answer.

I feel invisible. Is family destiny? If those interfaith and mixed-race Jews really don't affiliate, maybe I should just leave. Should I just hang up my kippah and join the atheists? I write this with some flippancy, because I know a good number of Jews who are also atheists. The truth is, I don't want to leave. Judaism was my first cultural home, and I intend for it to stay that way. Even when I have to fight to convince Jewish institutions that I belong.

I often use my own life as a counternarrative: an active and involved queer, mixed-race, Jew from an interfaith family. I do want more queer, mixed-race Jews from interfaith families to feel welcome in and connected to Jewish communities. But presenting myself that way—over and over and over and over again—actually leaves others with a two-dimensional version of myself. It sets up a paradigm of the good, involved queer, mixed-race Jew from an interfaith family and the bad, disengaged queer, mixed-race Jew from an interfaith family. It makes it sound like there is a formula: if Jewish communities are properly welcoming, then all queer, mixed-race Jews from interfaith families (or whatever minority of your choice) will become active and engaged Jews, fait accompli. This narrative flattens my own wrestling with how I—and many others—fit in the Jewish community.

For many years, my deep connection to the Jewish community has thrown into relief my lack of connection with my Chamoru culture. I thus sought a deeper knowledge of it in the only way I know how. The Jewish way. I have applied my years of Jewish study to my Chamoru culture. I tried asking my mom about what testimonies, statutes, and laws our culture commanded us, but I quickly discovered that the wise child of the Haggadah doesn't quite translate into Chamoru. I'm working hard to develop fluency in the language and understand the values. The most important is *inafa'maolek* (interdependence), but many are familiar: honoring elders, respecting and caring for the land, attending to the earth in her seasons. I have sat in on deep conversations about indigenous identity, protection of our land, and the ongoing harms of colonialism. For years I have explained to people that my family is Chamoru, the native people of Guam. But it took me two years of cultural learning before I could even, very hesitantly, say, Am I indigenous? Logically, the answer is clear. Chamorus are an indigenous people. I am Chamoru, so of course I am indigenous. I still struggle to say it, though. How can I position myself as belonging to a land and culture I know so little about? How can I own an identity that is thousands of years old and steeped in ritual and meaning? How is it that I have become the person questioning my credentials?

My internal monologue eerily mirrors the contingent membership I see enacted in the lesbian community. I have turned into my own interrogator, and over and over she asks me to prove that I belong. That demand to prove myself keeps me from being my true self as surely as the stereotypes of interfaith and mixed-race Jews do. But there is no need to interrogate people to determine their identities. To ask me to prove who I am cheapens our relationship. To put that desire aside makes space for you to learn who I really am, and for both of us to belong.

I am so much more than my labels. I do not carry some form of identification that can prove my qualifications, as a queer person, a Jew, or a Chamoru. My likes and traditions may look a little different than yours, but that does not make me less queer, less Jewish, less Chamoru. We would all be better off if we welcome those who show up and welcome them without question.

Chapter 5

Chelly Wilson

Lesbian, Holocaust Survivor, Queen of the Deuce

LAUREN HAKIMI

A Greek Jew with a Christmas tree. A lesbian who loved her husband dearly. A porn-theater owner who'd managed to leave Athens weeks after World War II broke out. Nowhere could Chelly Wilson have been all of these things except for Times Square, New York love-it-so-much-you-want-to-say-it-again New York.

Wilson was certainly a living paradox of a woman, but, like anyone, how people tell her story says more about them—and society as a whole—than it does about her. For example, a new documentary, *Queen of the Deuce*, brings the porn matron back into the public eye. The film, along with articles about it, portray Wilson as inspiring. They tell a story of an immigrant traumatized by the Holocaust who lifts herself up by the bootstraps to become lavishly wealthy and beloved, despite her multiple marginalized identities. While that narrative is true, anecdotes about Wilson's business dealings and how she viewed money suggest that inspiration shouldn't be the only takeaway.

Born in Salonika in 1908,[1] Wilson had a religious Jewish upbringing. Her dad arranged her marriage, and she resented it. "Every kiss he put on my body, I wanted to kill him," she said of her husband in an audio recording used in the film. "He was so repulsive to me, the son of a bitch."[2] After having two children, Wilson and her husband divorced. In 1939, war broke out in Europe, and Wilson knew that, as a Jew, she'd be killed if she stayed. She left Greece in a matter of weeks.[3]

In New York, at first Wilson sold hot dogs.[4] In 1941, she remarried— to a man, of course—and managed not to kill him.[5] "It was nice," Wilson said of her marriage with Jewish projectionist Rex Wilson. "He provided me with cigarettes."[6] She'd later have relationships with two women who also stayed in her apartment.[7] Wilson wasn't involved in porn yet, but she owned a theater where she showed Greek films. As business went well, Wilson raised money to send to the Greek army to support their anti-Nazi effort.[8] She also hosted Greek immigrants and helped them obtain legal status in the US.[9]

Salonika, the Greek city where Wilson was born, had such a large Jewish population it was nicknamed in Ladino *la madre de Israel*. When Jews were expelled from Spain in 1492, Salonika is where many of them moved. Sephardic Jews spoke (and still speak) a language that combined Spanish and Hebrew; the language, Ladino, would soon incorporate terms in Arabic, Greek, Turkish, and French, too, to reflect the languages of the Mediterranean, Middle Eastern, and North African countries in which its speakers once found refuge.

But Salonika was taken by the Nazis in April 1941. The Jewish population in Wilson's hometown was almost entirely annihilated. Miraculously, Wilson's children survived.

Wilson had lost custody over her son, Daniel, when she divorced her husband;[10] someone hid him in Salonika, and he later made it to Mandatory Palestine before he could be killed.[11] As for her daughter Paulette, Wilson had decided to leave her with a non-Jewish woman in Athens, possibly because she felt unable to be a good mother to her.[12] After World War II began, Wilson went back to the woman she'd left Paulette with and made her promise not to let anyone else take her.[13] Even when Wilson's own brother came to take Paulette to Salonika, the woman honored her promise to Wilson and didn't let him take her.[14] Because of this, Paulette would be one of few Jews who lived through the Holocaust in Greece and survived. After the war, Wilson had both Daniel and Paulette brought to the US to live with her and the daughter she'd had with Rex, Bondi.[15]

Meanwhile, as the market for Greek films declined, Wilson started showing porn and soon owned several theaters.[16] In Times Square, in midtown Manhattan, a new world of smut had emerged, thanks to thirsty GIs, evolving laws, white flight, and the changing character of the city.

The neighborhood, nicknamed "the Deuce," would soon be complete with sex workers, adult bookstores, illicit massage parlors, and peep shows. While politicians tried to use gentrification to reduce the area's violent crimes and put what they viewed as depravity to an end, Wilson stuck it out until the 1990s.[17]

In 1979 and into the eighties, a debate played out on the Deuce's streets, with radical feminist Andrea Dworkin and others arguing that porn was inherently antifeminist. Twice a week, the activist group Women Against Pornography gave suburban housewives guided tours of the neighborhood meant to raise awareness of what they viewed as the inherent violence of the scene.[18] Even Gloria Steinem and Bella Abzug marched through Times Square protesting against pornography.[19] But Wilson, for her part, didn't bother with such questions.

"She never had any compunctions about any of that. Couldn't care less about the content," said Wilson's son-in-law Don Walters, who was also involved in the film on the Deuce.[20]

Actually, Wilson did care about content; she wanted whatever content was most profitable. Articles attest that she asked filmmakers for more sexual content and hardcore close-ups, knowing they would sell;[21] a 1971 *Variety* article says she ordered cuts to films to avoid hassles with the district attorney.[22]

While Wilson and her husband were some of the first people to bring gay porn into New York City and produced more than fifteen gay porn films of their own, it might have been more of a financial calculation than a brave social stance; the city had a largely untapped market of gay porn consumers, whom the Wilsons charged more than they charged audiences for straight films. Wilson's husband told *Variety* magazine they did this to make sure audiences for gay porn had "class."[23]

"I think she loved the deal and making the deal more than she ever loved what the deal finally led to," Walters said.[24]

Many of Wilson's associates must have felt the same way, including mob members. Mafia capo Mickey Zaffarano came to her apartment for Friday night poker.[25] "Some of the stories I've heard say she was involved with the Mafia," said Wilson's granddaughter, Dina Pomeranz. "I think you had to be to be part of the pornography industry in the sixties and seventies."[26]

Mobsters dominated the Deuce; because of the scale of their operation and their willingness to use violent tactics, they were able to turn a profit despite police raids and other challenges inherent in the legally iffy world of porn and sex work. Wilson seems to have admired rule breakers, possibly because she lived in a world where—as a Jewish person, a woman, and a lesbian—rules were so unjust that one needed to break them just to survive. "She loved people who knew how to talk and get things done and sneak behind things and go around things. She just adored people like that," Walters said. "And unfortunately, she got involved with a few of them and got taken a bit from time to time, because they were good at it."

John Colasanti, who worked for Show World Center, a Times Square sex emporium, says that when he met Wilson, they hit it off—possibly because she liked being admired. "I think perhaps that's why she took a liking to me—because she saw the admiration I had on my face when I would speak to her," Colasanti said in the *Queen of the Deuce* film.[27]

Wilson was also accused of cheating people out of their money. "We had to deal with her, but she was a little cunt," said pornographic film-maker Phil Prince in an interview with the *Rialto Report*, a Deuce-themed website run by amateur historians. (Of course, when Prince calls Wilson a "cunt" here, he is using the language of sexist intimidation to chastise her for violating gender norms; it's more acceptable for businessmen to behave in a "cunt-like" manner than for businesswomen to do so.) "She was cheap, man," Prince added. "No one liked her."[28]

Film producer Arthur Morowitz said that in 1965, Wilson took advantage of his inexperience to charge him a very high price to adver-tise the film he'd invested in. It was "a very typical Chelly kind of deal," Morowitz said.[29]

They say all's fair in love and war—did Wilson believe the same to be true in business? Maybe Morowitz should've researched reasonable advertising costs. After all, porn was a business for people who could handle it. In other words, one can imagine how someone in Wilson's position might've justified her approach to business.

The documentary has a strange final scene featuring Wilson's grand-son, filmmaker David Bourla, who says his grandmother's story inspires him. "If you're not here to create something or to give someone else escapism or have a message or do something, then what are you doing?" he says.[30] It's a strange note to end on, since all available evidence suggests that Wilson didn't care about creating anything, at least not anything artistic.

A *New York Post* article says Wilson "embodied the American dream."[31] But if realizing this dream means treating business like a game that must be won at all costs, what is that achievement really worth? We live in a country of people so desperate for uplift and human-interest stories that it's hard to find an instance where the media mentions a Holocaust survivor without including the word *inspiring* next to it. Often, it's as if, no matter how much potential a story has for insight into society or culture or history, its value lies in whether or not it makes the person consuming it feel better. But what if Wilson—Holocaust survivor, immigrant, pioneering businesswoman—isn't actually inspiring?

Maybe, when a person doesn't fit in somewhere, as Wilson didn't anywhere, they hook up with others who don't fit in either, not bothering to measure which parts of them don't fit into what and why. If she were born ninety years later, would Wilson have had different values? Would she have waved from a float at her local dyke march, dissing the patriarchy and white Christian nationalists at every turn, aligning herself with pride and liberation rather than with mafiosi and other ill-defined troublemakers, whose trouble could be good or bad depending which way the wind blew?

There's no way to answer these questions. But it's worth wondering what happens when a person is placed in the position of needing to always justify themselves. They just might learn to justify other things, too.

Notes

An earlier version of this essay appeared in *New Voices* magazine.

1. Sara Stewart, "The Secret Life of Times Square's Notorious Porn Queen," New York Post, November 10, 2022, https://nypost.com/2022/11/10/the-secret-life-of-times-squares-notorious-porn-queen/.

2. *Queen of the Deuce*, dir. Valerie Kontakos (Exile Films / Storyline Entertainment / ERT, 2022), 17:44–20:12.

3. *Queen*, 22:40–24:03.

4. *Queen*, 25:02–35.

5. Curtis Russell (media contact for *Queen of the Deuce*), email message to author, November 9, 2022.

6. *Queen*, 30:12–31:16.

7. *Queen*, 57:41–58:00.

8. *Queen*, 29:42–30:10.

9. *Queen*, 41:55–42:19.

10. *Queen*, 20:30–41.

11. *Queen*, 32:16–33:35.

12. *Queen*, 20:43–21:19.

13. *Queen*, 22:40–23:31.

14. *Queen*, 26:27–27:00.

15. *Queen*, 32:16–36:15.

16. "Chelley Wilson, Queen of N.Y. Porno Exhibs, into National Distribution," *Variety*, February 17, 1971.

17. *Queen*, 1:08:21–29.

18. Anthony Bianco, *Ghosts of 42nd Street: A History of America's Most Infamous Block* (New York: HarperCollins, 2004), 4.

19. Barbara Basler, "5,000 Join Feminist Group's Rally in Times Sq. against Pornography," *New York Times*, October 21, 1979, https://www.nytimes.com/1979/10/21/archives/5000-join-feminist-groups-rally-in-times-sq-against-pornography.html.

20. *Queen*, 55:46–52.

21. Elena Gorfinkel, "Microhistories and Materiality in Adult Film History, or the Case of Erotic Salad," *Journal of Cinema and Media Studies* 58, no. 1 (2018): 150; " 'Deep Sleep' (1972): How a Suburban Porno Set Off a Massive Federal Witch Hunt—Podcast 52 (Reprise)," *Rialto Report*, transcript uploaded February 9, 2020, https://www.therialtoreport.com/2020/02/09/deep-sleep-3/; Troy Howarth, *Unholy Communion: Alice, Sweet Alice, from Script to Screen* (Orlando, FL: BearManor Media, 2021), 187.

22. "Chelley Wilson."

23. Addison Verrill, "Wilsons Hate All but Profit," *Variety*, April 1, 1970, 27.

24. *Queen*, 11:10–18.

25. *Queen*, 48:20–31.

26. *Queen*, 48:49–58.

27. *Queen*, 6:06–59.

28. "Avon Films: Journeys into the Dark Heart of XXX—Part 3, The Director," *Rialto Report*, December 16, 2018, https://www.therialtoreport.com/2018/12/16/phil-prince/.

29. *Queen*, 44:30–46:00.

30. *Queen*, 1:14:55–16:56.

31. Stewart, "Secret Life."

References

"Avon Films: Journeys into the Dark Heart of XXX—Part 3, The Director." *Rialto Report*, December 16, 2018. https://www.therialtoreport.com/2018/12/16/phil-prince/.

Basler, Barbara. "5,000 Join Feminist Group's Rally in Times Sq. against Pornography." *New York Times*, October 21, 1979. https://www.nytimes.com/1979/10/21/archives/5000-join-feminist-groups-rally-in-times-sq-against-pornography.html.

Bianco, Anthony. *Ghosts of 42nd Street: A History of America's Most Infamous Block*. New York: HarperCollins, 2004.

"Chelley Wilson, Queen of N.Y. Porno Exhibs, into National Distribution." *Variety*, February 17, 1971.

" 'Deep Sleep' (1972): How a Suburban Porno Set Off a Massive Federal Witch Hunt—Podcast 52 (Reprise)." *Rialto Report*, February 9, 2020. Transcript. https://www.therialtoreport.com/2020/02/09/deep-sleep-3/.

Gorfinkel, Elena. "Microhistories and Materiality in Adult Film History, or the Case of Erotic Salad." *Journal of Cinema and Media Studies* 58, no. 1 (2018): 147–52. https://muse.jhu.edu/article/705276.

Howarth, Troy. *Unholy Communion: Alice, Sweet Alice, from Script to Screen*. BearManor Media, 2021.

Queen of the Deuce. Directed by Valerie Kontakos. Exile Films / Storyline Entertainment / ERT, 2022. 77 min.

Stewart, Sara. "The Secret Life of Times Square's Notorious Porn Queen." *New York Post*, November 10, 2022. https://nypost.com/2022/11/10/the-secret-life-of-times-squares-notorious-porn-queen/.

Verrill, Addison. "Wilsons Hate All but Profit." *Variety*, April 1, 1970.

Chapter 6

Anniversaries

(2018–2021)

JOY LADIN

1. Abney Garden Park Cemetery

I rest on a bench
between leaning crypts

undermined and overgrown
by hawthorn roots and ivy,

making myself at home
among eroding angels

and moss-blurred epitaphs.
You're in your element,

snapping photographs,
deciphering grandiloquent expressions

of love, virtue, faith in resurrection.
Goldcrest and chiffchaff

wing from branch to branch.
Brevity and brilliance,

grief and acceptance,
in a single sun-struck glance,

surrounded by fungi—slime molds, jelly ears,
yellow brains, blushing rosettes—

fattening on Victorian arsenic and lead
in the hollowed-out trunks

of this urban forest
that meant to be a garden.

The pandemic won't start for a couple of years,
so it's easy to feel

life has triumphed over death,
overgrown and walled it in,

arranged it into artful paths,
resting places, granite slabs,

snippets of wilderness.
This is the perfect place

to feel how tired I am,
surrounded by nineteenth-century dissidents

and species that have trembled for decades
on the lip of extinction

like hairs in a thinning mustache.
Rustle and thud

in the underbrush.
I smile back at you across the graves.

Not me. Not here. Not yet.

2. Winter Anniversary

Wings of an angel
with two hearts

and two heads,
we lean out the window

into a night
cold, familial, and fragile

as the cheek of a mother
made of glass.

It's the night after the night
you came back.

Moonlight bright
as fresh-fallen snow

glories the frozen grass.

3. Sheltering in Place

waiting for corn to sprout, lilacs to open,
white supremacy to be dismantled

and the apolitical
whiteness of clouds

to inch across the sky;
for sleep to spread

from your leg to mine;
for the dog to tell us

pizza's arrived;
for notebooks to fill

and characters to become lives
and words that aren't mine

to arrange themselves
into the voice of the divine;

for cities to reopen,
treatments to work,

blood to fill
the right-hand chamber of my heart

even when I'm upright;
for chipmunks and buzzards,

black squirrels, snapping turtles,
great blue herons, mockingbirds, and foxes;

for something that feels like summer
to remind us

of shades of green we have forgotten
and phosphorescent insects to rise

from the grounds of the house
that isn't ours

to the story we inhabit,
the story of Sabbaths

lingering in the sky,
spooning bodies, caramelized onions,

gusts of rain through window screens;
symptoms that don't subside;

walks I can no longer take;
flashes of firefly.

4. When You're in New York

You walk through the world and I walk too,
shrinking and stretching inside your shadow,
glinting like sun on your glasses.

A bus is kneeling at a shelter
and look, I'm the shelter
and also the driver

kneeling thoughtfully in case you want to enter
then roaring off
through the city that loves you

almost as much as I do,
posing for your pictures, trying to look familiar,
trying to look brand new,

leading you through turns and tunnels
to the treasures cloistered
in the oldest layers,

rocks and shells and bits of paper,
bones and wounds
I want you to discover.

Whatever I have been or done
is yours.
You're the center of my map,

the sun I bask in beside the turtles,
the neighborhood I grew up in,
the little place

no one else will ever find
where you and I
are drinking wine

and falling in love again.

Chapter 7

The Sephardic Palimpsests of Emma Lazarus

Leonard Stein

Introduction

The legacy of the Jewish American poet and activist Emma Lazarus (1849–1887) has been reduced to a few lines from a sonnet affixed to the Statue of Liberty in the US that, over the past century and a half, shaped an American ethos: "Give me your tired, your poor, / Your huddled masses yearning to breathe free." While reminding us of a nation's imperative to embrace immigrants seeking refuge, these transcendent lines have obscured the strong, independent Sephardi woman behind them. In recent years, Lazarus has also been embraced and reread in queer and feminist studies for producing poetry about homoerotic desire.[1] This essay aims to elucidate the infrequently discussed later phase of Lazarus's creative exploration into her Sephardic heritage. I argue that Lazarus's creative engagement with Jewish literature of medieval Spain helped inform her inchoate lesbian voice. Like a palimpsest—a written manuscript that bears traces of an earlier text underneath it—Lazarus's poetry collapses the time and space separating the modern Sephardic diaspora from a medieval homeland. By reading, translating, and rewriting Hebrew literature accessible to her, Lazarus found a nexus of ambiguity, same-sex desire, Jewishness, and writing, all articulated as a Sephardic heritage rooted in medieval Spain.

Born in New York to a prosperous sugar refiner, Emma Lazarus was a fourth-generation descendent of the first Jewish community in the United States. Her great-grandfather led the first synagogue in the country, Shearith Israel, which was built by the Spanish and Portuguese community in the mid-seventeenth century. Her family's affluence allowed for Lazarus's adequate tutoring and the means to establish a literary career as a precocious teenager. With a thorough education in the classics and the poetics of the day, Lazarus would later experiment with various poetic forms and translations before her early death at thirty-eight. As a fierce proponent of Jewish heroism, she also wrote historical dramas to encapsulate contemporary political problems. Toward the end of her career, her poetry conveyed an unabashed prophetic voice. She advocated on behalf of disenfranchised Russian Jews and was one of the first US writers calling for a Zionist return to the Holy Land.

This essay begins with a brief overview of Hebrew poetry during the Muslim reign of al-Andalus, which I argue influenced the homoerotic poetry of Lazarus. Her manuscript poem "Assurance," specifically, has ignited critical reception in lesbian studies, which I review in the subsequent section. Offering a new critical direction, I then compare "Assurance" with forms of Andalusian homoerotic poetry that Lazarus translated into English. The similarities between medieval and modern texts produce a palimpsestuous queer reading that situates a Sephardic identity in her writing. By *palimpsestuous*, I refer to a neologism coined by French scholar Philippe Lejeune to convey the "reappearance of the underlying script" in a palimpsest; additionally, the term's evocation of the word *incestuous* "makes the concept of the palimpsest strange in a way that rewrites and refigures it in the context of late-twentieth and early twenty-first century literary and cultural thought," such as queer theory.[2] Lazarus's Sephardic identity not only stems from the Hebrew poets of al-Andalus but extends to a broader conception of Spanish Jewry. In the chapter's final section, I examine Lazarus's poem "An Epistle," as it similarly incorporates homoerotic imagery to portray the historical relationship of Jewish men in late-fourteenth-century Christian Spain.

Homoeroticism in Andalusian Poetry

The Prussian-raised Reform rabbi Gustav Gottheil, of New York City's Temple Emanu-El introduced Lazarus to German translations of the "golden age" of Andalusian Jewish poetry. In 1877, he had asked Lazarus to translate into English three by poems by Shelomo Ibn Gabirol, Moshe Ibn Ezra, and Yehuda Halevi. These poems were eventually published in a collaborative work in 1887 as *Hymns and Anthems Adapted for Jewish Worship*, one of the first books of Jewish hymns published in America. Despite her lack of Hebrew proficiency, Lazarus was fluent in French and German, having already printed translations of Heine as a teenager. German critical translations of the Andalusi Hebrew poets had been produced a generation earlier by scholars of the European *Wissenschaft des Judentums* (Science of Judaism), a movement broadly responsible for initiating the modern academic study of medieval Hebrew literature. The discovery of secular and liturgical Andalusian poetry propelled Lazarus to continue researching and translating more poems after delivering the requested English translations. First published in Jewish periodicals in 1879, her additional translations of Andalusian poems became part of a collection of pieces published in 1882 under the brave title *Songs of a Semite: The Dance to Death, and Other Poems*.

By consulting the works of *Wissenschaft* scholars to learn and rewrite her own heritage as a Sephardi, Lazarus would in turn discover a genre of Hebrew homoerotic poetry that would further influence her development as a poet. As with most of the poetry generated by Jews living as a minority in Muslim al-Andalus, lyrical homoeroticism derived from pre-existing conventions of Arabic poetry that traveled westward from major Arab cultural centers by the ninth and tenth centuries. For example, we find in Hebrew Andalusian poetry an acculturation to traditional wine poems. These works not only celebrated the courtly debauchery of garden and palace gatherings predominantly occupied by men, with their encouragement of drunkenness and exaggerated descriptions of their drink, but also lauded the beauty of the cupbearer, often a boy or a woman dressed as one. In the mid-tenth century, the first Jews to write Hebrew poetry in al-Andalus imitated the secular style and meter of the Arabic wine poem, which included objectification of the male subject.

The issue of Hebrew homoeroticism has been the subject of considerable and ongoing contention in the century-long scholarship on Hebrew medieval literature. Specifically, the florid descriptions of masculine subjects, composed by Jewish men during the golden age of Andalusian poetry (ca. 950–1150), has provoked a debate on the implications of actual homosexuality at this time. Virtually every significant scholar of medieval Hebrew poetry over the last century and a half—from Samuel David

Luzzatto to Jefim Schirmann to Raymond Scheindlin—has commented on the subject. In turn, scholarship has been mixed on the literary phenomenon of male speakers yearning for and sensually describing young men. Some critics have dismissed the masculine object as a stand-in for women or God; others liken it to a simple imitation of Arabic style; yet others consider homoerotic poetry to be historical evidence of social norms that differ what from what is often taught as Jewish male sexuality.[3]

Lesbian Desire in the Poetry of Lazarus

The divergent critical opinions on Andalusian homoeroticism highlight the ambiguity of reading and interpreting this poetry. This ambiguity directly served Lazarus, a modern Sephardi, similarly interested in blurring distinctions of gender in her own erotic poetry. As in the case of the Andalusi poets, the question of Lazarus's sexuality has long intrigued and frustrated biographers and critics. Apart from overreading her lifelong bachelorhood, no evidence exists to substantiate what had long been hinted at in her writing. Nevertheless, Lazarus has become somewhat of a celebrated figure in feminist and queer scholarship as an early Jewish American, English-language poet whose writing appears to limn same-sex desire.

Lazarus's poems "Magnetism" and "Venus of the Louvre," for example, sensually describe female figures through the desires of a speaker; the speaker of the former poem is consumed with "the red flame in my blood, / By my nerves' electric thrill," and that of the latter is "dazzled" by an "enthralled enchantress."[4] Perhaps due to the impossibility of explicit lesbian intimacy in Lazarus's time, these poems illustrate the temporal and physical displacement that separate the speaker from her objects. In "Magnetism" the speaker confronts a haunting ghost, while in "Venus" the poet Heine encounters a classical statue. Both poems deny the possibility of actual sexual union. Furthermore, Zachary Turpin has recently republished lesser-known poems by Lazarus that originally appeared in *Lippincott's Monthly Magazine*. These works, Turpin asserts, read "as confident, public expressions of queer desire."[5] Still, women in these poems are portrayed as vanishing siren-mermaids or lying corpses that deny the possibility of intimacy between Lazarus's speakers and her objects of desire.

One poem, however, goes furthest in depicting a potential lesbian union. This work has generated a wave of critical attention—more than any other piece of Lazarus's writing—in efforts to categorize Lazarus as a queer or lesbian poet. The mystery of the poem's origins, its discovery, and the unusually explicit sensuality of the text likely contributed to its mystique and its placement in various anthologies of erotic poetry. Shortly before her early death in 1887, Lazarus ensured the preservation of her life's work by meticulously organizing and transcribing approximately ninety of her favorite poems in a notebook. This collection was later used by her sisters to publish the posthumous, near-exhaustive two-volume collection *The Poems of Emma Lazarus*. However, one manuscript poem, titled "Assurance" above its cursive text, was bowdlerized by the Lazarus sisters and went unnoticed by scholars for nearly sixty-five years. In 1951, a doctoral student named Arthur Zeiger consulted the archived notebook for his dissertation on Lazarus, providing the first transcription and critique of the poem. Zeiger's publication of "Assurance" began a series of interpretations that parallel the contentious claims made by Hebrew scholars about medieval homoeroticism.

Assurance

Last night I slept, & when I woke her kiss
Still floated on my lips. For we had strayed
Together in my dream, through some dim glade,
Where the shy moonbeams scarce dared light our bliss.
The air was dank with dew, between the trees,
The hidden glow-worms kindled & were spent.
Cheek pressed to cheek, the cool, the hot night-breeze
Mingled our hair, our breath, & came & went,
As sporting with our passion. Low & deep
Spake in mine ear her voice:
    "And didst thou dream,
This could be buried? this could be asleep?
And love be thrall to death! Nay, whatso seem,
Have faith, dear heart; *this is the thing that is!*"
Thereon I woke, and on my lips her kiss.[6]

The poem is a Petrarchan sonnet (fourteen iambic pentameter lines with the rhyming pattern *abba, cdcd, efef, aa*), filled with enjambment (sentences flowing beyond one line), with lush natural settings, a dramatic suggestion of death, and adventurous passion. In this, it fits Lazarus's style of romantic poetry. The subject—an assertive, undeniably female lover—and her unusual relationship with the speaker might or might not hint at an autobiographical lesbian romance. In his dissertation, Zeiger offered a "Freudian examination" of Lazarus, claiming that the poet's bachelorhood and "abnormally strong attachment to her father" helps designate the poem as "a lesbian fantasy."[7] Dan Vogel, in his reading of "Assurance," rejects Zeiger's conflation of poet and speaker. Vogel noted that "it would not be the first time that Lazarus presumed to speak the passion of a man."[8] Indeed, in the poem Lazarus does not explicitly signal that the speaker is female.

Esther Schor follows Zeiger's lead by claiming the poem provides a glimpse into Lazarus's "unconscious." Schor argues that the poem is not about a mysterious lover in her biographical life but "about being chosen by desire—erotic desire, and for the body and soul of a woman."[9] Most recently, in *Queer Expectations: A Genealogy of Jewish Women's Poetry*, Zohar Weiman-Kelman asserts that features of the poem comprise a "model of lesbian history, where . . . the lesbian is neither entirely present nor absent, neither present nor past."[10] Weiman-Kelman notes that while Lazarus conceals the speaker's gender, the poem's "clitoral imagery" in the mating female fireflies, the irregular rhyme scheme, the use of reinforcement instead of the expected *volta* (the closing turn of a poem), and even Lazarus's deliberate act of not dating the poem in her notebook (unlike her other entries) make this work such a model.[11]

The above readings illustrate how a single poem can spark a spectrum of critical interest still animated by the mystery of the poet's *sexual* identity. Nevertheless, no critic, to my knowledge, has considered the way in which Andalusi poets generally informed a homoerotic sensibility in Lazarus's writing, most clearly articulated in "Assurance." Such a discussion will further queer readings of the poet specifically rooted in her Sephardic identity, as Lazarus's writings and outward expressions of herself as Jewish can be similarly read in terms of difference and ambiguity.

While a strong defender of Jewish values and heritage, Lazarus stood out as a celebrity outlier in an era unfamiliar with Jewish secularism. In fact, she once confided to her friend Ellen Tucker Emerson that the Lazarus family had become "outlawed now, they no longer keep the Law, but Christian institutions don't interest her either."[12] Lazarus was too markedly Jewish in her professional life to assimilate into a socially Christian mainstream—titling her poetry book *Songs of a Semite*. Yet she was also too messianic in her proto-Zionism for the developing Reform Jewish movement in America. Furthermore, she was too removed from observance for her family's multigenerational membership in the Orthodox Spanish and Portuguese congregation. In all, Emma Lazarus's alterity can just as readily be traced along Jewish lines as along sexual orientation.

Reading "Assurance" through Andalusian Homoeroticism

Lazarus was familiar with homoerotic poetry from al-Andalus and included several examples of it in her published English translations. Indeed, it appears that a translated Andalusian poem influenced the composition of "Assurance." To use the metaphor of the palimpsest, the product of a text written over an earlier text underneath it—the latter referred to as a hypotext—we can refer to medieval homoeroticism as hypotext to Lazarus's sensual poetry. The particular hypotext to "Assurance" appears in *Songs of a Semite*, where Lazarus introduces the translated poetry of Shelomo Ibn Gabirol with two epigraphs, the first an untitled laudatory poem by Moshe Ibn Ezra:

> Am I sipping the honey of the lips?
> Am I drunk with the wine of a kiss?
> Have I culled the flowers of the cheek,
> Have I sucked the fresh fragrance of the breath?
> Nay, it is the Song of Gabirol that has revived me,
> The perfume of his youthful, spring-tide breeze.[13]

Ibn Ezra's poem, as translated into English by Lazarus, suggests an unmistakable similarity to the manuscript poem "Assurance." In both short poems, a speaker addresses a desire presumably for the same sex, conjuring "lips," a "kiss," a "cheek," a "breath," and a "breeze"; the speaker questions an intimate encounter and interjects with "Nay," leading to a climax of their awakening by way of the lover's words. In the metaphor of the palimpsest, Lazarus writes over Ibn Ezra's "Song of Gabirol" to produce the original poem "Assurance." Underneath the "Song," however, rests another text, produced by the *Wissenschaft* scholar Abraham Geiger. It was Geiger's German translation of the poem in his 1867 book *Salomo Gabirol und seine Dichtungen* that served as Lazarus's source text for her English translation:

> Schlürft' ich der Lippen Honig ein?
> Berauschte mich des Kusses Wein?

Hab' Wangenblüthen ich gepflückt,
Gesogen Athems frischen Duft?—
Mich hat Gabirol's Lied erquickt,
Sein Aushauch junger Frühlingsluft.[14]

Like Lazarus after him, Geiger turned Ibn Ezra's lines into a call-and-response by posing the opening metaphors as questions. Aside from adding the speaker's "Nay" as an answer to the preceding questions in the poem (e.g., "Am I sipping the honey of the lips?"), Lazarus generally follows Geiger's translation. Underneath this layer of Geiger's German translation rests yet another layer, that of the original text of the Andalusian Hebrew poem:

נֹפֶת שְׂפָתַיִם וְיֵין שִׁנַּיִם / אוֹ צִיץ לְחָיַיִם וּמֹר אַפָּיִם

אוֹ נָשְׁבוּ רוּחוֹת נְעוּרִים מִפְּאַת / מִכְתַּב שְׁלֹמֹה תַּאֲוַת עֵינָיִם

Is it honey on the lips and wine of the teeth
    or the blossoming of cheeks or breath of myrrh?
Or have winds of youth blown from
    Shelomo's letter, a delight for the eyes.[15]

Geiger's translation veered significantly from the original Hebrew, most egregiously by misattributing the name of the subject in the poem.[16] Despite Geiger's editorial interventions, Lazarus still incorporated the original Hebrew poem's rhetorical features for her own writing. This intertextual influence between medieval and modern poetry again evokes the metaphor of the palimpsest. Sarah Dillon has suggested that the metaphor can release a "palimpsestuous queer reading," which "traces in the fabric of literary and cultural palimpsests the interlocking narratives of 'masculinity' and 'femininity,' 'heterosexuality' and 'homosexuality' that characterize gender and sexual identity, writing and culture."[17] Dillon directed her critique at the modernist bisexual writer H.D., who juxtaposed the lesbian desire of modern female characters with settings in ancient Egypt and Rome. The emphasis of difference underlying a model of queerness manifests in H.D.'s writing through layers of temporality and gender. A similar model can apply to Lazarus's medievalist writing, in which a temporal and spatial collapse between al-Andalus and Lazarus's modern New York and the shift from male to female homoeroticism establish an intimate interaction between broader systems of writing.

To offer a palimpsestuous queer reading of "Assurance" by examining the Andalusian poetry first conveyed in Lazarus's published translations thus opens new directions of criticism that extend beyond familiar investigations into the poet's biography. Specifically, interwoven with Andalusian homoeroticism, "Assurance" incorporates rhetorical devices used by Andalusi poets. For example, Ibn Ezra's Hebrew poem uses a conventional Arabic rhetorical device known as *tajāhul al-'ārif*, or "feigned ignorance," in which the speaker hyperbolically questions his perception of reality. So overwhelming are the emotions for his subject that the speaker confuses metaphors with the object to which they apply.

Similarly, Lazarus's poem primarily projects a queering ambiguity by questioning the existence of a shared experience. In "Assurance," the speaker tersely juxtaposes experiences unclearly real or fantasized until the tension climaxes toward an answer ("Am I sipping the honey of the lips? . . . Nay"). The speaker has slept, yet feels a kiss when she wakes, and so the dream of walking with a woman through a glade (and whatever other activities the scene implies) appears as an exaggerated impossibility and yet feels real. The term "feigned ignorance" implies that the medieval poet or speaker clearly understands the distinction between the literal and the metaphorical and that the rhetorical questions posed stylistically emphasize the exaggerated degree of feeling toward the subject. Despite the fear that "love be thrall to death," the speaker's account of the experience in waking life indicates a discernment of the reality of her emotions.

In addition to the echo of *tajāhul al-'ārif* highlighting the ambiguity of a homoerotic experience, "Assurance" also exhibits a motif known as *ṭayf al-khayāl*, or "phantom spirit." Developed throughout early and medieval Arabic literature and incorporated by the Andalusi Jewish poets, *ṭayf al-khayāl* involves the beloved encountering the speaker—like a phantom—in the haunting and arousing experience of a dream. Select lines from the eleventh-century Saragossan poet Yosef Ibn Ḥasdai's "Orphan Poem," an ode dedicated to fellow poet and Granadan vizier Shemuel Hanagid, elaborately illustrate the motif in the way Lazarus eventually appropriates it:

וְשָׁכַבְתִּי—וּבֵין שָׁדַי קְוֻצּוֹת מְרִיקוֹת מֹר עֲלֵי רַקָּה אֲדֻמָּה

וְהַיָּמִין מְחַבֶּקֶת לְבָנָה וְהַשְּׂפָה מְנַשֶּׁקֶת לְחַמָּה

וְהַמִּטָּה מְקֻטֶּרֶת לְבוֹנָה וְהָעֶרֶשׂ בְּכָל בֹּשֶׂם פְּטוּמָה.

וְנָעַמְתִּי בְחֶזְיוֹנִי, עֲדֵי כִי הֲקִיצוֹתִי—וְהִנֵּה אֵין מְאוּמָה

אֲבָל רֵיחַ יְשׁוֹבֵב הַנְּפָשׁוֹת וּמֹר עוֹבֵר יְחַיֶּה הַנְּשָׁמָה

And I lay down—and between my breasts, curls
dripping with myrrh over reddened cheeks

And [my] right hand embracing the moon
  and my lips kissing the sun
And the bed perfumed by frankincense
  and our couch filled with fragrance
And I delighted in my vision, until
  I awoke—and behold, there was nothing
Only the scent that brings back life
  and flowing myrrh that revives the soul[18]

The descriptions of the fellow poet operate within a dream fantasy that resembles the hazy imagery and dramatic climax in Lazarus's "Assurance." Like the lovers in "Assurance," elements of nature enmesh with body parts (hair, lips, cheeks) until the speaker awakens. Again like "Assurance," the speaker here awakes with no trace of the lover, only a reviving scent—not unlike the perfumed "spring-time breeze" in Lazarus's translation of Ibn Ezra. Both "Assurance" and Ibn Ḥasdai's "Orphan Poem" bring the intensity of the lover's dream to a climax that coincides with a sensual awakening.

The ṭayf al-khayāl exemplifies a lover's only resource for encountering their beloved; the motif of dream-hauntings often appears in contexts of irreversible separation, such as the beloved's death, their departure from the city, or a dissolution of the relationship. For "Assurance," we may add a new scenario, that of the impossibility of an open romance between two women. The creation of the beloved in the faculty of *imagination*, as the medieval Arab logicians understood it, or the *unconscious*, as modern critics would phrase it, allows the speaker in "Assurance" an interiorized experience through the representation of the absent woman.

Medieval Masculine Writing versus Modern Female Orality

As previously mentioned, Lazarus placed the Ibn Ezra poem as the first of two epigraphs to introduce her English translations of Ibn Gabirol's poetry in *Songs of a Semite*. The second epigraph, a quotation from Ibn Gabirol, illustrates an important distinction in the use of homoeroticism by the Hebrew male poets mentioned thus far versus that of Lazarus: "I will engrave my songs indelibly upon the heart of the world, so that no one can efface them."[19] The line imagines an ultimate hypotext, in which Ibn Gabirol boasts that his words go beyond their permanent markings on parchment and into the heart of the world, "so that no one can efface them." The metaphors of engraving and effacement, of course, hearken back to the concept of the palimpsest, etymologically derived from the ancient practice of scraping written text on a wax tablet for reuse. Likewise, the medieval poems in Lazarus's translations play with conventions of same-sex desire through the textual metonymy of *writing*. For Lazarus, however, a song, such as a "Song of Gabirol," assumes an alternative meaning: art expressed orally.

Unlike the passions symbolized in the penetrating hands and letters of erudite medieval men—what Hélène Cixous might dismiss as phallogocentric—Lazarus offers a palimpsestic layering of sensual experience through the mouth and speech of modern women. The wondrous effects of a poem, first detailed in self-reflexive Andalusian poetry, shift in the female poet's rendering from a textual to an oral experience. In another metaphor for the palimpsest, the subject of "Assurance" addresses the speaker's fear that their shared ethereal moments might "be buried." But through a voice "low and deep," the speaker *hears* of its indelibility, offering the poem's namesake, the spoken words "*this is the thing that is.*" Like a palimpsestic text, the existence of a hidden, buried layer emerges when encountering the superficial layer; in this case, the poem's inclusio (i.e., its bookending phrase) recalls the speaker's awakening with the lover's kiss, "still floated on my lips." A dreamy escapade, in other words, has been *impressed* upon the speaker and recalled through a kiss, an intimate receipt connecting past with present. The awareness of the kiss reifies the experience of what came before it and what, like the amnesia that follows dreaming, threatens to fade away.

Homoeroticism in Lazarus's "An Epistle"

The Jewish legacy of same-sex desire that influenced "Assurance" would also inform for Lazarus a conception of Sephardic writing that extends beyond the Andalusian period. The mystical eroticization of orality—in figurations of the mouth, lips, breath, and voice and the words they produce—reappears most vividly in Lazarus's creative translation of a wholly different era in medieval Spanish Jewry. In 1391, amid anti-Jewish riots and massacres that spread throughout Catholic Spain, the Jewish scholar Shelomo Halevi of Burgos converted to Catholicism, becoming Paulus de Santa Maria. Shortly afterward, his former student, Joshua Joseph Ibn

Vives Halorki, penned a letter trying to make sense of how an admired leader could abandon his people. Inspired by *Wissenschaft* historian Heinrich Graetz's summary of the epistle, Lazarus composed thirty-four ottava rima stanzas (i.e., each stanza contains eight iambic pentameter lines and has the rhyming pattern *abababcc*) that imagine its impassioned, confused, and sarcastic contents.

As with "Assurance," the long medievalist poem contains multiple layers underneath Lazarus's English text: first, the original late-fourteenth-century Hebrew letter; second, Graetz's description of that letter in his survey *Geschichte der Juden*, the source for Lazarus's reconstruction of the manuscript. In the epistle, published in the same period as her other "Jewish Poems," Lazarus temporally collapses Christian Spain into an Andalusian poetic sensibility by projecting a homoerotic tension onto Halorki and his converted teacher, Paulus de Santa Maria. In the beginning stanzas of the letter, for example, Lazarus imagines Halorki's sense of betrayal while recalling the days when the two men would leave the synagogue where Paulus used to teach:

> For on the Synagogue's high-pillared porch
> Thou didst hold session, till the sudden sun
> Beyond day's purple limit dropped his torch.
> Then we, as dreamers, woke, to find outrun
> Time's rapid sands. The flame that may not scorch,
> Our hearts caught from thine eyes, thou Shining One.
> I scent not yet sweet lemon-groves in flower,
> But I re-breathe the peace of that deep hour.
>
> We kissed the sacred borders of thy gown,
> Brow-aureoled with thy blessing, we went forth
> Through the hushed byways of the twilight town.
> Then in all life but one thing seemed of worth,
> To seek, find, love the Truth. She set her crown
> Upon thy head, our Master, at thy birth;
> She bade thy lips drop honey, fired thine eyes
> With the unclouded glow of sun-steeped skies.[20]

Echoing verses from "Assurance," the speaker nostalgically reminisces about a relationship through their experience together in nature. Again, we read of a couple's stroll away from the city, where the sky glows (here from a setting sun, instead of glowworms), and the sense of awakening that disrupts their previous experience (being rapt in the synagogue). Lazarus also conveys homosocial intimacy through expressions of the mouth. The teacher shines because of his oral sermons, and the speaker "re-breathe[s] the peace" from their twilight together. More evocative are the lips, which sublimate a typically erotic signification for a religious purpose. The speaker kisses the "sacred borders of thy gown," a reference to the custom of kissing ritual fringes worn underneath the clothing of Jewish men. Universally practiced by the wearer, the custom here teases the speaker's propinquity to naked skin.

The startling images of lips that "drop honey" echoes Lazarus's Ibn Ezra translation "sipping the honey of the lips," both borrowed from the Song of Songs: "Nectar your lips drip, bride, honey and milk are under your tongue" (4:11). To situate this metaphor in the speech of a rabbinic student conjures the classic midrash, which equates the erotic image of sweet lips to words of the Torah expounded by rabbinic sages, "sweet like honey to those who hear it" (Shir Rabba 4:11). But these lines also reflect the coded language of a scorned lover writing from the pain of nostalgia. By converting to Catholicism, the beloved has replaced the speaker for another man—a false messiah of all things—who, as Lazarus startlingly declares by the end of the letter, is no more a god than a decayed, flaccid worm amidst other worms (in contrast to the bioluminescent mating of glowworms in "Assurance"). This betrayal manifests, as in the way of lovers, through the lips: what first uttered the pleasurable words of the Torah and revived the speaker now screeches an anti-Jewish rhetoric that, in fact, kills.

Conclusion

The above examples, "Assurance" and "An Epistle," illustrate the way Lazarus's creative translations informed her development as a poet, a process probably ignored by critics because of the alloyed results of translating Hebrew indirectly from German. Nevertheless, what started as a favor for Gustav Gottheil to translate a few poems for his book on Jewish hymns burgeoned into a personal project of understanding who these ancestral Spanish Jews were. As a result, the medieval poets provided Lazarus a resource to identify a heritage not strictly defined by religious grounds. Andalusian poetry offered some of the language to express what likely reflected her own romantic interests. By incorporating aspects of the translations into her original poetry, Lazarus constructed Sephardic palimpsests that offer new directions for critically reading ambiguous homoeroticism.

Notes

1. See, for example, her inclusion in Zohar Weiman-Kelman, *Queer Expectations: A Genealogy of Jewish Women's Poetry* (Albany: State University of New York Press, 2018); Noam Sienna, *A Rainbow Thread: An Anthology of Queer Jewish Texts from the First Century to 1969* (Wynnewood, PA: Print-O-Craft Press, 2019); and Meredith Stabel and Zachary Turpin, eds., *Radicals: Audacious Writings by American Women, 1830–1930*, vol. 1, *Fiction, Poetry, and Drama* (Iowa City: University of Iowa Press, 2021).

2. Sarah Dillon, *The Palimpsest: Literature, Criticism, Theory* (London: Bloomsbury, 2007), 4–5.

3. On the critical reception of Andalusian homoeroticism, see Leonard Stein, "My Heart Is in *Sepharad*: Writing Medieval Spain in the Modern Sephardic Diaspora" (PhD diss., University of Toronto, 2021). For a range of scholarship on the subject in English, see Jefim Schirmann, "The Ephebe in Medieval Hebrew Poetry," *Sefarad* 15 (1955): 55–68; Raymond P. Scheindlin, *Wine, Women, and Death: Medieval Hebrew Poems on the Good Life* (Oxford: Oxford University Press, 1999); Norman Roth, " 'Fawn of My Delights': Boy-Love in Hebrew and Arabic Verse," in *Sex in the Middle Ages: A Book of Essays*, ed. Joyce E. Salisbury, 157–72 (New York: Garland, 1991).

4. Emma Lazarus, *The Poems of Emma Lazarus*, vol. 1, *Narrative, Lyric, and Dramatic* (Boston: Houghton, Mifflin, 1889), 185, 203.

5. Zachary Turpin, "Yearning to Breathe Free: Emma Lazarus's Queer Innovations," *J19* 4, no. 2 (2016): 421.

6. Emma Lazarus, *Emma Lazarus: Selected Poems and Other Writings*, ed. Gregory Eiselein (Peterborough, ON: Broadview, 2002), 96.

7. Arthur Zeiger, "Emma Lazarus: A Critical Study" (PhD diss., New York University, 1951), 192.

8. Dan Vogel, *Emma Lazarus* (Boston: Twayne, 1980), 89.

9. Esther Schor, *Emma Lazarus* (New York: Schocken, 2006), 233.

10. Weiman-Kelman, *Queer Expectations*, 88.

11. Weiman-Kelman, 85.

12. Edith Emerson Webster Gregg, ed., *The Letters of Ellen Tucker Emerson*, vol. 2 (Kent, OH: Kent State University Press, 1982), 225.

13. Emma Lazarus, *Songs of a Semite: The Dance to Death, and Other Poems* (New York: American Hebrew Publishing, 1882), 66.

14. Abraham Geiger, *Salomo Gabirol und Seine Dichtungen* [Solomon Gabirol and his poems] (Leipzig, Germany: Oskar Leiner, 1867), 63–64.

15. Moshe Ibn Ezra, *Shirei ha-ḥol* [Secular poetry], vol. 1, ed. Haim Brody (Jerusalem: Schocken, 1934), 96.

16. Geiger substitutes the "Shelomo" in the original Hebrew text for "Gabirol" in the German translation, as if Ibn Ezra was writing about the famous Andalusi poet Shelomo Ibn Gabirol. In fact, he was corresponding with an Almoravid physician in Seville, Shelomo Ibn al-Mu'allim. In reading Geiger, Lazarus perpetuated the misattribution, inserting the poem as an introduction to the poetry of Ibn Gabirol.

17. Sarah Dillon, "Reinscribing De Quincey's Palimpsest: The Significance of the Palimpsest in Contemporary Literary and Cultural Studies," *Textual Practice* 19, no. 3 (2005): 257.

18. Jefim Schirmann, *Ha-shirah ha-aivrit bi-sefarad u-ve-provans* [Hebrew poetry in Spain and Provence], vol. 1 (Jerusalem: Mosad Bialik, 1954), 173; my translation. The medieval poem appears in its entirety in various Hebrew publications and translations. See Schirmann's anthology for additional commentary on Ibn Ḥasdai's poem as well as other Andalusian homoerotic poetry.

19. Lazarus, *Songs*, 66.

20. Lazarus, *Emma Lazarus*, 219.

References

Dillon, Sarah. *The Palimpsest: Literature, Criticism, Theory*. London: Bloomsbury, 2007.

———. "Reinscribing De Quincey's Palimpsest: The Significance of the Palimpsest in Contemporary Literary and Cultural Studies." *Textual Practice* 19, no. 3 (2005): 243–63.

Ibn Ezra, Moshe. *Shirei ha-ḥol* [Secular poetry]. Vol. 1, edited by Haim Brody. Jerusalem: Schocken, 1934.

Geiger, Abraham. *Salomo Gabirol und Seine Dichtungen* [Solomon Gabirol and his poems]. Leipzig, Germany: Oskar Leiner, 1867.

Gregg, Edith Emerson Webster, ed. *The Letters of Ellen Tucker Emerson*. Vol. 2. Kent, OH: Kent State University Press, 1982.

Lazarus, Emma. *Emma Lazarus: Selected Poems and Other Writings*. Edited by Gregory Eiselein. Peterborough, ON: Broadview, 2002.

———. *The Poems of Emma Lazarus*. Vol. 1, *Narrative, Lyric, and Dramatic*. Boston: Houghton, Mifflin, 1889.

———. *Songs of a Semite: The Dance to Death, and Other Poems*. New York: American Hebrew Publishing, 1882.

Roth, Norman. " 'Fawn of My Delights': Boy-Love in Hebrew and Arabic Verse."
In *Sex in the Middle Ages: A Book of Essays*, edited by Joyce E. Salisbury,
157–72. New York: Garland, 1991.

Scheindlin, Raymond P. *Wine, Women, and Death: Medieval Hebrew Poems on
the Good Life*. Oxford: Oxford University Press, 1999.

Schirmann, Jefim. "The Ephebe in Medieval Hebrew Poetry." *Sefarad* 15 (1955):
55–68.

———. *Ha-shirah ha-aivrit bi-sefarad u-ve-provans* [Hebrew poetry in Spain and
Provence]. Vol. 1. Jerusalem: Mosad Bialik, 1954.

Schor, Esther. *Emma Lazarus*. New York: Schocken, 2006.

Sienna, Noam. *A Rainbow Thread: An Anthology of Queer Jewish Texts from the
First Century to 1969*. Wynnewood, PA: Print-O-Craft Press, 2019.

Stabel, Meredith, and Zachary Turpin, eds. *Radicals: Audacious Writings by
American Women, 1830–1930*. Vol. 1, *Fiction, Poetry, and Drama*. Iowa
City: University of Iowa Press, 2021.

Stein, Leonard. "My Heart Is in *Sepharad*: Writing Medieval Spain in the Modern
Sephardic Diaspora." PhD diss., University of Toronto, 2021.

Turpin, Zachary. "Yearning to Breathe Free: Emma Lazarus's Queer Innovations."
J19: The Journal of Nineteenth-Century Americanists 4, no. 2 (2016): 419–24.

Vogel, Dan. *Emma Lazarus*. Boston: Twayne, 1980.

Weiman-Kelman, Zohar. *Queer Expectations: A Genealogy of Jewish Women's
Poetry*. Albany: State University of New York Press, 2018.

Zeiger, Arthur. "Emma Lazarus: A Critical Study." PhD diss., New York University, 1951.

Chapter 8

Remembering Sinai
A Spoken-Word Midrash

SABRINA SOJOURNER

Many of us took in those who wanted shelter or were simply scared to be alone.

Introduction

The text we have been given for the Torah and the Tanakh is a deeply male-oriented telling of our story as a people. Yet, all along the way, there are indications that there is another perspective—a deeper, more inclusive perspective—regarding the less textually documented role of women in our development into a nation of priests and, arguably, priestesses. What are the ways in which we look at our stories, our text, and limit how far we are willing to stray to contest the context in which women are seen and assessed—even by women?! How do we fail to name the jealousy many early male commentators had of us? How do we miss the hints that are in the Torah, ignoring the biased male commentaries? When do we go beyond the commonly taught stories to find the jewels that seek to balance and counter some of the noise? More importantly, how do we move beyond our education and indoctrination to create a different narrative regarding the assumed power dynamics of the canon?

I did not begin to write "Remembering Sinai" with these questions in mind. I began with a simple assignment: Tell the story of receiving Torah to a group of people with varying levels of Jewish education, varying intellectual abilities, and the span of Jewish practices. I did not know at the start that I would be writing women into our story. I certainly did not know that I would give a nod to the deeper relationships of women without all the labeling we carry, for better or worse, today.

Though I do not mention skin color anywhere in this piece, I want to make clear: The people of the Tanakh are not "White." Race is a fiction invented by Christian commentators and later weaponized by popes, kings, and other authorities to justify war against foreign continents to kill, maim, and enslave people in non-European lands and loot their treasuries and cultures.

The history of the Jewish people is the history of modern humans. We were among those who moved out of East and South Africa and flooded the world.

Lastly, this commentary, this S'Torah Telling (Lab Shul) is intended to be read aloud—even if you are alone. If you are part of a group, there is guidance for discussion at the end of the midrash. However you discover this piece, may you experience blessings for your journey!

ON TRANSLITERATION

For those unfamiliar with the term, transliteration is the use of the "Latin" alphabet (the letters you are reading) to approximate a word's pronunciation in Hebrew. In this text, there are words written in Hebrew with their transliteration in parenthesis, followed by their English translation.

CONSONANTS

The letters ח and כ are represented by *kh*.
The letters כ and ק are represented by *k*.
א and ע are indicated with '.
ה is represented with an *h*, even when it is silent.

VOWELS

A is pronounced "ah," as in *father*.
E is pronounced "eh," as in *red*.

Ei or *ey* is pronounced "ā," as in *eight*.
I is pronounced "ee," as in *see*.
O is pronounced "oh," as in *crow*.
U is pronounced "oo," as in *moon*.
Ai is pronounced as in *I* and *aye*.
Lastly, *Sinai* is a transliteration of the Hebrew and is pronounced
  "Seen-aye."

Remembering Sinai

Alive in me is the terror of the horrors that hit all of us.

Alive in me is the shock and the confusing wonder—awe—I felt when they only hit the Egyptians!

Alive in me is the anticipation that grew into excitement as we prepared for the first פֶּסַח (*pasakh*), the sacrifice. We culled our many flocks for the best lambs, placed them in small pens within the public squares amid our homes. They had plenty to eat and drink. We did nothing to harm them. We allowed our children to brush, pet, water, and feed the sheep. It was unexpectedly difficult to explain to our youngest child that we planned to kill the sheep for food. We told him that our care and attention would allow the lambs to be calm when it was time to offer them as sacrifice.

Thankfully, there were no temples dedicated to Amun in Goshen.[1] Only the Amun priests would have cared about why we had so many lambs in our midst. Most others among the Egyptians had no desire to wander into our spaces.

When it was time, I untied the lamb for our family. Our children, my beloved, and I walked our lamb to the pit. My sons and daughters-in-law were already at their pits near ours. I sat on a stool next to the pit, and the ram sat next to me. The youngest and I petted him. Soon his head was in my lap, and he rested peacefully. He started to struggle as my beloved tied his back haunches, but we cooed and kept petting him. Only when he was blissfully calm did we say the blessing and make a deep, quick cut to the throat and hoist him up. We collected the blood as directed.

I was among those checking doorposts. We didn't want anyone missed. But there were some . . . I think only a few . . . who did not want the blood on their doorjambs. They thought us טִפְּשִׁי (*tip'shi*) silly:

עוֹבֵד אֱלִילִים (*oveyd eylilim*) pagan—no better than the Egyptians.

לֹא קָמִיעַ עַל-שְׁתֵּי הַמְּזוּזֹת (*lo kamia al-shtei ham'zuzot*) no protection on the doorpost!

Alive in me is the beauty of our feast, being carefree as we packed and danced and sang. I can feel the voices of women laughing, singing, and chanting in my aching heart. I close my eyes longing to remember those notes. The feeling is strongest when I pick up a תוֹף (*tof*), a hand drum, allowing my fingers to wander over the surface however they wish.

While many ate in their homes, more of us ate communally. There was something about sharing everything. Singing songs, trying to remember the old stories.

We walked around, making sure all ate, including those who worked alongside us, often helped us, and their families. It was a joyous, festive meal and there was plenty, and nothing could be leftover.

We took in those who wanted shelter or were simply scared to be alone, and then it was time. Fires out. Doors and windows closed.

And I remember . . . especially during certain types of windy storms . . . there is a howling that arises . . . surrounds me . . . Is that human wailing? or a wind shrilling as it moves quickly through a tiny crack? a low, moaning wind exploring crevices, or human moans of distress?

I can only tell the difference when I bring my mind to now. Then, I am certain it is a distant soul memory of my mother wailing as she awakened to find my father dead . . . the wailing of others who did not take protection, mixed with the howling of the Egyptians who did not have protection from the last and final wondrous sign that was our miracle.

I remember the joy that broke through my grief when the news came that we were to leave immediately! I gathered my mother, my family, and all who were ecstatic to leave misery behind!

Yes, we did stop at the houses of Egyptians to gather items from them. Mostly, we reclaimed what was once ours: Gifts given to them centuries ago when relations were good. Items taken from us when our status changed. Many items made with our hands for which we were not compensated. There were items that celebrated our heritage: candlesticks, goblets, and platters, including those of Yoseif and As'nat and the rest of that generation; bread bowls that belonged to our ancient mothers, tapestries and fabrics woven over centuries by our hands that reminded us from whom we were descended, and yarns we spun from the best wool and flax.

We also remembered the bones of Yoseif! The Egyptians knew we could not leave without them and tried to hide them from us. But Serakh Bat Asher[2] knew that the Egyptians had placed Yoseif's bones in an iron sarcophagus and tossed it into the deep silt of the Nile in hopes that we would never find them. The Egyptians had underestimated the power of El Shaddai and that of Serakh Bat Asher! She knew! She knew.

Serakh Bat Asher took Moshe to the spot and called to Yoseif's bones to rise up. "Bones of Yoseif, son of Rakhel and Ya'akov! Rise up! It is time to take you to the land of your mother and father." The entire delta could hear her, and we chanted with her:

Rise up, bones of Yoseif, son of Rakhel! Rise up!
Rise up, bones of Yoseif! It's time to take you home.
Rise up, bones of Yoseif, son of Ya'akov! Rise up!
Rise up, bones of Yoseif! It's time to take you home.
Rise up, bones of Yoseif, son of Rakhel! Rise up!
Rise up, bones of Yoseif! It's time to take you home.
Rise up, bones of Yoseif, son of Ya'akov! Rise up!
Rise up, bones of Yoseif! It's time to take you home.
Rise up, bones of Yoseif, son of Rakhel! Rise up!
Rise up, bones of Yoseif! It's time to take you home.
Rise up, bones of Yoseif, son of Ya'akov! Rise up!
Rise up, bones of Yoseif! It's time to take you home.
Rise up, bones of Yoseif! Rise up!
Rise up, bones of Yoseif! It's time to take you home!
Rise up, bones of Yoseif! Rise up!
Rise up, bones of Yoseif! It's time to take you home!
Rise up, bones of Yoseif! Rise up!
Rise up, bones of Yoseif! It's time to take you home!

And rise up they did! The waters of the Nile bubbled as she chanted, and the river spit that iron sarcophagus into the air, and the Blessed One caused it to land right at their feet, open! Serakh Bat Asher and Moshe gathered Yoseif's bones, carefully wrapping them with an additional purple shroud. Then joined Aharon and Mir'yam and all the families at the front to lead us out and away from Mitzrayim! I don't remember who cheered louder: the Egyptians or us!

I remember worrying about my mom. The only time she seemed to smile was when our younger children were crawling all over her or a baby was near. So, we made sure there was always a child or a baby that needed to be held or fed or patted to sleep in her arms or lying close to her. Between our youngest children and my grandchildren—her great-grandchildren—it was easy and seemed to help, but I continued to worry until . . .

Until one night, as I was cooking, Ima started humming a song, and tears moved through me so quickly, I bit my lip to keep from weeping aloud. I swayed as she hummed, remembering all the times Ima sang that song to me and my siblings to calm us, to aid us in sleeping. Later that night, my husband and I joined her in singing all the little ones to sleep. It was not long before the song was ringing through the camp. Do you remember?

B'shem El Ro'i, Elohei Yisrael	לְאֶרָשִׂי יְהֶלְאֶ יוּר לֹא מֹשֶׁבְּ
Mimini Mikhael, umismoli Gavriel	לְאֵירְבַּגְ יְלְאמֹשְׂמוּ, לְאֲכָימְ יְנִימִימְ
Umilfanai Uriel, umei-akhorai Rafael	לְאֶפְךָ יְרוֹחֲאֶמֵי, לְאֵירוֹא יְנַפָּלְמוּ
V'al roshi, Shechinat-El	לֹא תְנִיכְשִׁ יִשָּׁארֵ לֶעֻ

In the name of El Ro'i, the God of Israel
On my right Michael, on my left Gavriel
In front of me Uriel, behind me Rafael
And o'er my head, surrounding me Shekhinat-El.

I remember when we finally arrived and encamped by the Sea. We had been moving day and night, resting here and there. It had been days since we left Mitzrayim. We were just beginning to settle in when word arrived from those in the back that there was a dust cloud as high as the sky and as wide as the horizon and thundering in the ground. We all knew it was Pharaoh and his army coming to take us back to our nightmare. We cried out to El Shaddai, and some wasted their time complaining to Moshe. I watched Moshe's face. He didn't seem surprised. I found that strangely reassuring.

Did you see it? Did you? Tell me you saw the Angel of El Shaddai move the Pillar of Cloud from in front of us to behind us; and with her went clouds that formed over and around us and descended behind and between Pharaoh and us. The thundering stopped, and we waited . . . and we waited . . . Night began to rise, and though we could not see the sky, we could still see each another. Do you remember? Small fires appeared throughout our encampment, for seeing and for cooking. The Egyptians could not bother us, and we had no desire to bother them.

Like yourselves, my family and I settled in for the evening. I brought out my bread bowl and added more flour and water to what was there, working the dough until it was soft, compliant, and fragrant.

I grabbed small handfuls and formed them into balls, flattening and stretching them several times before tossing each on the cook stone.

I so loved watching my children and my husband making a game of predicting which will puff first, letting them know it was time to turn it over. Though not as festive a meal as the one the night before we left, every bite was beyond delicious because it was a meal in freedom! And with our El Shaddai's help, I knew it would not be our last.

I know that's what allowed me to fall soundly asleep in the arms of my beloved, our young children close to us. The older ones with their families huddled close, and Mom was in the middle with the babies. No matter what the morning brought, we would still be free. El Shaddai had brought us this far, and I believed that El Shaddai, the Most High, would not release us to go back. Whatever our future, it was not in Mitzrayim.

Well before dawn, the order moves through camp that we need to be ready at sunrise and not a moment later. As the dark begins to recede, the fires dim at the same pace until they disappear as magically as they appeared.

The breath of El Shaddai blows and the Sea . . . The Sea! More vast than I remember from the night before. Louder! It all feels more danger-ous . . . I am so terrified I cannot find my voice.

Then, my husband, my Nakh'shon, takes a few steps into the Sea. I want to scream "What are you doing?" and nothing comes out of my mouth. He stops and turns back, smiling. He stretches out his left hand for me. His eyes, his eyes! Shining as bright as the day I first saw him.

As then, I grab his hand, and together we reach out our arms for our children and their families, our oldest ones helping their grandmother. Together, we take more steps. Every step terrifying, yet there is no turn-ing back.

Our trust is rewarded! All the water recedes, including that in our clothing! The water forms walls high on each side of us, higher than anything we or others had built for any Pharaoh! We walk on dry land to the other shore.

Once on the other side, we self-organize so there is plenty of room. All of us make it safely. Not one soul is left behind.

Then, we watch . . .

It's still hard to fathom. You see, well behind the last of us, Pharaoh's army entered the water. When the last of them entered the Sea, we were all safe. We watched the water walls crumble and crash on them. Horses and men and chariots churned . . . then this eerie calm.

All gone! Who knows how many! On the other side of the Sea, a lone figure upon a horse was all that remained.

Then, we understand! We realize the miracle El Shaddai has performed for us, and we raise our voices to the Most High! We are laughing and crying. Nakh'shon picks me up and twirls me around like a man half his age. We laugh! What a joyous laugh! As he puts me down, I turn, and there is my sisterfriend and love,

Mir'yam! We take a moment and just hold each other. I know her grin matches my own, and we know exactly what to do! We grab our *tofim*,[3] twirl around, and chant:

"We just lived a miracle! We are dancing!"

A roar rises, and soon other women, including Ima and Elisheva, join us in chanting and singing praises to the Holy Oneness of El Ro'i!

Our El rescued us!
There is no el like our El!
All the wonders! All the miracles!
We are singing and dancing praises to our El!

We sing, chant, and dance well into the night. The fire of El Shaddai does not dim and neither does our energy. We rest the next day, and the day after that we resume our journey to El's Holy Mountain.

We are such a funny people. For weeks we witness miracles almost daily, and yet there are always those who are not satisfied. Fortunately, our El loves us. So, when there was an uproar about bitter water, the healers sweetened it with bitter wood. When there was an uproar about a lack of food, which there was not, the Most High caused dew to appear on the ground and produce לֶחֶם מִן-הַשָּׁמַיִם (*lekhem min hashamayim*)—bread from heaven: a miraculous food! There is always enough, and it tastes exactly like whatever I am craving. Personally, I was happy not to have to cook. It's a lot of work!

For most of us, the journey was also about our growing trust: our trust in each other and our trust in our El. We were becoming one people. We were becoming El Shaddai's people, and the proof that we were almost ready was our arrival at Har Sinai, and I remember . . .

It is the first day of the third month after our exodus from Egypt when we reach B'mid'bar (wilderness) Sinai and camp near the Eternal One's mountain.

Many of us know we are near before it is announced. We are suddenly flooded with memories of stories, swirling with the memories of all the miracles and wonders we experienced in Mitzrayim flood each of us...

There's something about knowing one is close to holiness. I always weep. With joy and trepidation, I always weep.

We have just finished setting up our tents when word arrives that Moshe is summoning the elders. So, Nakh'shon, our two eldest, and I leave everything with Ima.

Moshe shares the message from El Shaddai. More than that, he tells us all the stories of our people from the beginning of the Universe to this very moment. We are weeping. It is the cry of relief. Now we know for certain that this is the Holy One of our Mothers and Fathers returning us, bringing us to be proximate, and to be special. "You shall be to Me a nation of priests and priestesses," the Eternal says through Moshe, "My Holy Nation and My Holy People."

We, the council of elders, answer as one voice and one mind:
כֹּל אֲשֶׁר-דִּבֶּר אֵל שַׁדַי נַעֲשֶׂה (*Kol asher diber El Shaddai na-ase!*)
Everything El Shaddai says, we will do!

I think our eagerness pleased El Shaddai, who spoke to Moshe again, saying we were to wash our garments, meaning we got a chance to bathe. On the third day, El Shaddai would descend before the eyes of all of us upon Har Sinai.

All who want to help work to set clear boundaries so that no one will ascend the mountain nor touch its edge. We want to protect our children, elders, and animals should they wander and accidently touch the mountain. No one can touch the Eternal's mountain and live. We have to wait for the ram's horn's long, sustained blast. Only then can we ascend the mountain.

I remember the third day dawning with thunder rumbling across the sky and lightning charging the air ... turning my gaze to the Mountain and seeing heavy clouds hanging over it. The shofar sounds low. Distant. Steady.

Is it my fear I'm feeling or that of my *kahal* (community)? I think it is both. It's all ...

I mindfully dress. With our families, Nakh'shon and I join the throng. A loud blast startles all of us. Still, when Moshe motions to us, we follow him out of the camp.

We reach the foot of Har Sinai and arrange ourselves just outside the boundaries surrounding the mountain, many times our numbers. The mountain is completely covered with smoke, with fire. There is heat and nothing that would hurt us. A wind keeps the smoke from us. I find it confusing and wonderful.

We must all be here, for the long blast sounds and grows louder as the mountain unexpectedly quakes. I feel . . . unsure . . . it's all amazing . . . and scary . . . I see the fire and the cloud and feel the shaking . . . I hear the thunder and see the lightning, though my eyes are closed. It is all so far away and yet so close. The shofar grows louder!

I squeeze Nakh'shon's hand, and he pulls me to him. We hold onto each other. I feel us thinking the same thought: If either of us lets go, we are both lost . . .

The quaking is frightening, yet a voice rises within, and I/we say: Yes, we hear you!

A voice rises within, so loving, so freeing, and I/we say: Yes, YES! We love you!

We are separate and yet we are not. It's wonderful and so puzzling!

I remember a time when I thought it was just a strange and sweet dream I dreamed repeatedly, periodically throughout my life. Then one Shabbat afternoon, in a Torah study group, we were reading Deuteronomy and the dream memory of being part of an expanse flooded my body; being in the air suspended with people across, above, and below; moving, being moved through something I still do not understand! A silence so loud it was calming. A light so bright—if you only saw it with your eyes, you would call it fire! Feeling fear and not being afraid—that's awe! That's awe! Love! Love so big, so huge, so unending I still weep in gratitude.

Alive in me is the memory of being on the Eternal One's mountain with people I loved.

I look at your faces, and my heart remembers you. When I see you with my heart, remembering, reexperiencing the Eternal's Sinai, I reexperience that deep, unshakable, overwhelming love!

That's the message of Sinai! We are love and we are loved. We are loved and we are love!

This is the message of Sinai, of Khorev: We are love and we are loved. We are one with The One. We are One.

ת Alive in me is the memory that we are One.

Gratitude

I am deeply grateful to all my readers and commentators, especially Ann Thompson Cook, Yavilah McCoy, Nancy Slater Weiss, Minna Sherlinder Morse, Amy Winn, Abby Gondek, Tamara Fish, Justin B. Terry-Smith, Dr. Marsha Darling, Rabbi Rain Zohav, Rabbi Lauren Holtzblatt, Martin Lewin, and Ada Gold.

I am also thankful for conversations with Anthony Mordecai Tzvi Russell that aided my musical approach.

Early audiences and students that provided invaluable feedback were the Revitz House Residence Association, Selah 15, and the Jewish Women of Color Resilience Circle 1.

Please handle this document with care, as it contains names for the Divine One.

Process for Discussion

PAIRS: ACTIVE LISTENING

Look the speaker in the eye and have a pleasant countenance on your face. What is your immediate reaction, impression, response?

Two minutes each, thirty-second warning. Thank each other and switch. Thirty-second warning and switch.

SMALL GROUP: CONTINUE ACTIVE LISTENING MODEL

What, if anything, was

> new?
> surprising?
> challenging?
> affirming?
> confusing?

Fifteen minutes, being mindful of hearing from everyone in your group. Two-minute warning.

Dedication

This work is lovingly dedicated to the inaugural Jewish Women of Color Resilience Circle sisterhood: Amani Hayes-Messinger, Anike Tourse, Autumn Leonard, Rebecca "Beckee" Birger, E. M. Walker, Kavitha Kasargod-Staub, Keyanna Silverman-Maddox, Rabbi Mira Rivera, Noé Hakim-Sefarty, Oraneet Shikmah Orevi, Rachel Faulkner, Rebecca Jaye, Samiah Fulcher, Sara Goldberg, Sarah Waisvisz, Sheba McCants, Tikva Nadia Womach, and Tonda Case. And to our amazing conveners, teachers, and facilitators, Yavilah McCoy and Lisa Anderson. Each of you caused me to realize my journey has been to know that I am precious.

Notes

1. The lamb was the symbol of Amun, a major Egyptian deity. Egyptians in the know would have been offended to know that the lambs were to be sacrificed, especially for a deity that was not Amun. Some linguists claim that the name is also the origin of *Amein/Amen*.

2. Serakh was the daughter (*bat*) of Asher, one of Ya'akov's sons by Zil'pah, Leah's handmaiden. Zil'pah also bore Gad. Serakh is the only daughter from that generation mentioned in the Exodus genealogy.

3. Plural of *tof* (hand drum).

References

"B'Sheim HaShem" (adapted). *The Standard Prayer Book*. Translated by Simeon Singer. New York: Bloch Publishing, 1915.
Sh'mot/Exodus 6:1–20:23.

Chapter 9

Life on the Borderlands

Mizrahiut, Transfemininity, and Stateless Diasporas

A. S. Hakkâri

Within Jewish spaces, Mizrahi Jews are often treated both as the most authentic Jews and as lesser, "barbarous" Jews. Within transfeminist circles, the transfeminine experience is often described as "a man when it hurts us, a woman the rest of the time." Within MENA[1] communities in the diaspora, Kurdish inclusion is contingent on a silencing of our histories. Our lives are undeniably shaped by our Womanhood, Jewishness, and Orientalization, but our narratives exist at the contested edges of these identities. This experience of a "borderland identity,"[2,] as I have come to call it, often makes us targets both within the broader society and within our own communities and networks of support.

An often-used definition of *Mizrahi* is "an Arab Jew" or, more charitably, "a Jew from the Arab world." Others sometimes narrow this definition further, defining *Mizrahi* as those MENA Jews (such as those who lived in the Ma'abarot) facing marginalization in the history of Zionism.[3] These definitions often fail to account for many Mizrahi communities, such as Jewish Kurds, Persians, and African Jews. In other cases, the terms are often contradictory in their application. If Mizrahi identity is defined by trauma in relation to Zionist efforts, where does that leave MENA Jews who were forcibly assimilated in their homelands but did not flee, or who chose to leave their homelands and immigrate to non-Palestinian lands? I plan to expand on the scholarship surrounding these definitions in the future, but here I will put forward my operational definition of *Mizrahi*: a Mizrahi Jew is an intracommunally orientalized Jew.

Milica Bakić-Hayden writes of Orientalism functioning like a set of "nesting dolls" in which communities positioned as being part of the "Orient" can themselves contain identities that are positioned as internal orients.[4] This fractal gradient of Orientalism is a useful analytical lens for studying the politics and histories of the region. This internal Orientalism can be seen in Turkey's treatment of its Kurdish population and its usage of propaganda positioning Turkey as a patriarchal and civilizing force.[5] Similar relationships exist within the civilizing projects of Baathist Iraq and Pan-Persian Iran. In much the same way, Mizrahi communities often recreate these internal Orientalisms. Kurdish Jews, upon immigration to Israel, often had their names Arabized to blend in with Arab Jews, exemplifying broader Orientalist ventures in a microcosm.[6]

This politics of naming often exhibits itself as a daily reality for those on the borderlands. In my case, when I came out of the closet at sixteen, I had internalized many of these politics, and this came through in my own self-naming. Although I chose a Kurdish name, in retrospect, I can't discount the significant appeal that my name's parallels in the languages of my colonizers may have had for my sixteen-year-old self. My position within these borderlands of identity affected even my act of self-determination as a trans person in a cisnormative world.

Trans women can be seen as residing within the borderlands of Womanhood. In 2011, a transgender woman from Tennessee was denied legal recognition as a woman. In protest, she stood topless outside the DMV that denied her gender-marker change. She was soon arrested on charges of public indecency, although the police report referred to her as a man.[7] Cisnormative society experiences and treats trans women as existing within the liminal space between male and female; we are consistently treated as whichever harms us more—even treated both ways within the same instance, contradictorily, as in the Tennessee DMV incident.[8]

This dual treatment typifies the societal reality of people impacted by transmisogyny.[9] Transgender women face higher rates of domestic and street violence, including sexual violence, in comparison to our cisgender counterparts. We face higher rates of homelessness, difficulty maintaining jobs, and medical malpractice, which we are forced to play into and accept, lest we be robbed of our bodily autonomy.[10] These statistics become even bleaker when combined with compounding factors such as family rejection. The most frequent depiction of us comes from pornography, which treats us as fetishistic fantasies for the sexual fulfillment of cisgender people rather than as whole individuals. On a more personal level, I have yet to meet another transgender woman who does not possess within themselves a complete and wholly defining fear. To exist as a woman within society is traumatizing, and to exist as an outsider to cis womanhood is doubly so.

When we are homeless, we are not allowed in women's shelters; when we stay in mixed-gender shelters or sleep on the street, we are assaulted or killed. When we are offered a job to elevate ourselves out of poverty, we are often forced back into the closet, made to choose our physical needs over our mental well-being.[11] Oftentimes, the only career path that allows us to exist as we are is sex work. Because of this situation, we are frequently forced to rely on community support and donations for even our most basic needs.

Because of our position as reliant on communal support, many trans women find ourselves trapped in whatever communities originally take us in. We are often asked to do labor for the community, and when we speak up about mistreatment, we are promptly disposed of under flimsy excuses.[12] The consequences of this can be more severe for trans women of color, especially Black transgender women.[13] When we use our lived experiences in organizing to break into the nonprofit sector, we are often given lower-ranking positions and asked to do labor far beyond the duties of our job. Many trans women, when expressing the depravity of the violence we face, hear cisgender women reply, "Welcome to womanhood." Our authenticity and our narratives as women are contingent on our trauma and our silence, our agreeing not to contradict cisgender women. This experience of conflict and conditional acceptance marks a borderland identity.

Similar experiences of poverty and exploitation are central to the story of my family as Kurdish refugees in diaspora. My mother fled to the US from the encroaching genocide of the Al-Anfal campaign.[14] One of my earliest memories is of myself in the bath, at age six or seven, as my mother washed my hair and told me that any day might bring the next Anfal. That duplicate apocalypse never came; instead, what followed was over a decade of Islamophobic and Orientalist violence in the wake of 9/11. The diaspora experience thus became a balancing act of politics and safety.

Diaspora communities of MENA ethnic minorities, such as the Kurds, are often small, and we are asked to set aside our pre-diasporic experiences for the sake of intercommunal solidarity and safety. It is a difficult choice; do you set aside your ancestral trauma for the sake of safety? For many of us, that trauma is as recent as our own parents, and it had an impact on every aspect of our upbringing. We are asked to accept that the violence of the Occident outweighs the violence of the homeland, and thus we are asked for tacit forgiveness of the crimes our parents faced. If we try to speak on the horrors of the Turkish, Iranian, and Baathist regimes, our new communities reject us, leave us to the proverbial wolves, and deny the protection and support of a larger community. Our new community denies our indigeneity to the region where we experienced violence, denies the existence of our communities denied, overwrites our histories, and frames us as foreign invaders of our own land.

Other people from neighboring diasporas treat these ideologies and histories as relics of an irrelevant past, despite the ever more dire situation for Kurds in our homeland. The past century of warring imperialisms has unwoven many aspects of our culture; even my own Kurdish, like my mother's, is interspersed with Arabic, Turkish, and Persian words. Because of this century of violence at the hands of nation-states, there has been a gradual schism in Kurdish politics; many have abandoned Kurdish nationalism entirely. Many Kurds instead focus on the occidental roots and nature of nation-states. Many of us advocate a future free of ties to nationalistic self-definition, where the gradient of culture that spans across the region is allowed to exist in its wholeness.[15]

At the same time, many of these Arab, Turkish, and Persian diasporic communities within the US predate our own, and community members often use the recency of our immigration to frame and romanticize us as possessing a more authentic experience. I have repeatedly spoken about my relationships with Yazidis, Alevis, and Kurdish Jews only to receive an awestruck expression from Arabs, Turks, and Persians. For many of these third- and fourth-generation immigrant communities, the Orient exists only as a nostalgic homeland, the Zion of their grandparents. Their authentication of our experience is a double-edged blade, however; our authenticity is bound up with our orientalization. We are of the Old World, mystical, mythical; we are outdated, superstitious, fictional. The ethno-racial hierarchies of our homelands, and their nesting orientalisms, have made the journey with us.

Existence on these edges of identity—simultaneously Jew and Gentile, male and female, authentically Oriental and foreign invader—positions us as subservient to the wishes and goals of each of these communities. We are subject to the same experiences and harm as others within our communities, but we are deprioritized for, and distanced from, support. Falling outside of the norm of marginalized identities—existing both as an example of and a challenge to the prevalent narratives in our community—incurs its own unique challenges and experiences. Our expertise in our own lives is always held as suspect, and we are always on the defensive, always struggling, always in contention; we are forever trapped in the borderlands.

Notes

1. The acronym *MENA*, short for Middle Eastern and North African, refers to the region as well as communities from that region.

2. After completing this piece, I was shown by a reader and editor the work of Gloria E. Anzaldúa and its similarities to my own ideas in both language and subject. I believe our works differ in that her writing seems to explore the societal borders between dominant and marginalized identities, especially in regard to chicano/a/x identity. My writing is targeted toward the people who exist within and between those established borders, especially within the Middle East and North Africa. However, the convergent development of our terminologies can also be seen as mirroring our similar experiences as colonized populations. The anti-national organizations of the YPG and YPJ (the so-called Rojava movement) and the Zapatistas in Chiapas have expressed solidarity with one another and regard one another as convergently developed sister organizations.

3. Ella Shohat, "The Invention of the Mizrahim," *Journal of Palestine Studies* 29, no. 1 (1999).

4. Milica Bakić-Hayden, "Nesting Orientalisms: The Case of Former Yugoslavia," *Slavic Review* 54, no. 4 (1995): 917–31, https://doi.org/10.2307/2501399.

5. Welat Zeydanlıoğlu, " 'The White Turkish Man's Burden': Orientalism, Kemalism and the Kurds in Turkey," in *Neo-colonial Mentalities in Contemporary Europe? Language and Discourse in the Construction of Identities*, ed. Guido Rings and Anne Iffe, 155–74 (Newcastle, UK: Cambridge Scholars Publishing, 2008). Zeydanlıoğlu's text and Bakić-Hayden, "Nesting Orientalisms," serve as a good introduction to the topic of localized Orientalisms.

6. "No sooner had he landed in the country than Israeli officials lopped off parts of the family's last name, the part that marked him as a Kurd. Beh Sabagha,

Aramaic for 'House of the Dyer,' would have been nonsensical in Israel. So, when they registered with immigration officials, his son Rahamim simply put down 'Sabagh.' That was Arabic for 'dyer' and a common name among Middle Eastern Jews. But Ephraim hadn't lived among Arabs, and Arabic had never been his language." Ariel Sabar, *My Father's Paradise: A Son's Search for His Family's Past* (Chapel Hill, NC: Algonquin Books of Chapel Hill, 2008), 112.

7. "Andrea Jones, Tennessee Transgender Woman, Goes Topless in DMV Protest," *HuffPost*, November 16, 2011, updated December 6, 2017, https://www.huffpost.com/entry/andrea-jones-transgender_n_1097978.

8. The trans woman interviewed summarizes the situation well, saying, "If I was a male, I had the right to, when I stepped out the door, take off my shirt. . . . It's not right for the state to ask me to be both male and female. A choice needs to be made. They cannot hold me to both standards" ("Andrea Jones").

9. *Transmisogyny* refers to the unique marginalization faced by transgender women and people interpreted by society to be transgender women—most centrally, CAMAB (coercively assigned male at birth) trans individuals.

10. Sandy E. James et al., *The Report of the 2015 U.S. Transgender Survey* (Washington, DC: National Center for Transgender Equality, 2016), 13, 96, 176, 248.

11. James et al., *Report*.

12. Porpentine [Charity Heartscape], "Hot Allostatic Load," *New Inquiry*, May 11, 2015, https://thenewinquiry.com/hot-allostatic-load/.

13. Dahlia Saint Knives, "V for Vendetta," *Medium*, April 1, 2020, https://medium.com/@thesaintknives/v-for-vendetta-453744c8d031.

14. The Al-Anfal campaign is the name for the genocide and ethnic cleansing of the Kurdish people carried out by the Baathist government in an effort to Arabize the perceived fifth column of the Kurdish people. The so-called "Kurdish question" and the historical status of Jewish people in non-Jewish lands are often cited as points of commonality and solidarity within both communities.

15. Abdullah Öcalan, a notable Kurdish political figure, writes about this fundamental incompatibility between the region and the modern imposition of nation-states, writing that "the national question is not a phantasm of capitalist modernity. Nevertheless, it was capitalist modernity which imposed the national question on society. The national society replaced religious community. However, the transition to a national society needs to overcome capitalist modernity if the nation is not to remain a disguise for repressive monopolies." Abdullah Öcalan, *The Political Thought of Abdullah Öcalan: Kurdistan, Woman's Revolution and Democratic Confederalism* (London: Pluto Press, 2017), 47.

References

Bakić-Hayden, Milica. "Nesting Orientalisms: The Case of Former Yugoslavia." *Slavic Review* 54, no. 4 (1995): 917–31. https://doi.org/10.2307/2501399.

James, Sandy E., Jody L. Herman, Susan Rankin, Mara Keisling, Lisa Mottet, and Ma'ayan Anafi. *The Report of the 2015 U.S. Transgender Survey*. Washington, DC: National Center for Transgender Equality, 2016.

Öcalan, Abdullah. *The Political Thought of Abdullah Öcalan: Kurdistan, Woman's Revolution and Democratic Confederalism*. Translated by Havin Guneser and International Initiative 'Freedom for Abdullah Öcalan—Peace in Kurdistan.' London: Pluto Press, 2017.

Porpentine [Charity Heartscape]. "Hot Allostatic Load." *New Inquiry*, May 11, 2015. https://thenewinquiry.com/hot-allostatic-load/.

Sabar, Ariel. *My Father's Paradise: A Son's Search for His Family's Past*. Chapel Hill, NC: Algonquin Books of Chapel Hill, 2008.

Saint Knives, Dahlia. "V for Vendetta." *Medium*, April 1, 2020. https://medium.com/@thesaintknives/v-for-vendetta-453744c8d031.

Shohat, Ella. "The Invention of the Mizrahim." *Journal of Palestine Studies* 29, no. 1 (1999): 5–20.

Zeydanlıoğlu, Welat. " 'The White Turkish Man's Burden': Orientalism, Kemalism and the Kurds in Turkey." In *Neo-colonial Mentalities in Contemporary Europe? Language and Discourse in the Construction of Identities*, edited by Guido Rings and Anne Iffe, 155–74. Newcastle, UK: Cambridge Scholars Publishing, 2008.

Chapter 10

Meeting Cicely, or Love and Politics

A Black Jewish Lesbian Memoir

CAROL CONAWAY

This segment from my memoir in progress introduces the lesbian dating scene in Boston in the 1970s amid the racist and classist challenges among lesbians and situates myself as a Black Jewish Lesbian, raised among the Black working class and battling mental illness. It was a tough time, and my story gives readers a glimpse into the issues faced by the various intersecting communities I was trying to navigate as I built a personal life as a young graduate student.

I'd barely entered my apartment before the phone rang. Although I was too tired to answer it, the ringing was persistent. I picked up the receiver and heard a familiar voice on the line.

"Carol? It's Tina. Where have you been?"

"I was at school." I answered her with some irritation since I wanted to be left alone to sit down and relax.

"Are you free tonight? There's a Newbury Street gallery opening. Why don't we go?"

"Sure. Let's go!" I responded eagerly because I knew the opening would be accompanied by free food and drink. I was strapped for grocery money.

We agreed that Tina would walk to my apartment and we'd go to the gallery together.

I'd known Tina since I'd moved to Boston from Philadelphia four years before, in 1973. We'd met at a lesbian party in Cambridge and hit it off immediately because we shared a couple of things in common: both of us were about to be thirty, and both of us were Jews. I was drawn to her because she was an artist. A native New Yorker, she had an air of sophistication that intrigued me. Her comings and goings were mysterious. She was as charismatic as I was shy. If it is true that opposites attract, we would have been a successful couple instead of being "just friends."

Tina arrived at my apartment as planned. When she entered my living room, she nodded approvingly. As she viewed the high ceilings, two fireplaces, large living room, and small bedroom, she was pleased with what she saw.

"How in the world did you find this great place? And how can you afford it? It overlooks the Charles River and the MIT part of Cambridge. If you don't mind my asking, how much is your rent?"

"Oh, I didn't find it. The white developers who renovated the building would never have shown this place to me. They'd have directed me to the Black ghetto. My ex was white. They were glad to have her sign the lease although she was unemployed. When she left me, I continued to pay the rent. My rent then was the same as it is now—$265 a month. Not a bad deal, huh?"

I loved bragging about my apartment because it was beautiful. My friends were wowed by it whenever they came for dinner, and that always pleased me. My place smacked of some level of wealth—or so I thought—and that made me very happy. Having grown up in a lower-middle-class neighborhood, I vowed I would never settle down in a poor neighborhood when I became an adult.

Now, I had made my vow a reality. My apartment was on historic Beacon Street in the Back Bay area. It was just a few blocks from Beacon Hill, a highly desirable address for those who were white and very wealthy. The Massachusetts State House, with its golden dome, was situated on Beacon Hill. The hill was close to Boston City Hall and the financial district. The state house, city hall, and the city's financial district formed the seat of power. I always was drawn to power. Having or being close to having power was my unfulfilled daydream.

We walked to the gallery, looked at a few of the paintings on display, ate some cheddar on little rounds of bread, drank a couple glasses of wine, and left as quickly as we could.

"Wow! That was one dreary opening!" exclaimed Tina. "And did you see the prices of his paintings? Highway robbery. Let's go back to your place and have a drink. That will help ease the pain of our having wasted the better part of the evening."

Once at my place, Tina asked me about my Bostonian social life.

"Who else do you know of our 'persuasion?' Are you just going to live alone forever like a hermit? You need to get out and meet some gay people. By that I mean women. You need to rejoin GPW. Get over your rage about how they treated members that didn't fit their definition of 'Gay Professional Women,' Carol."

"I'm sure the membership wasn't happy that I joined. They considered themselves too liberal to ignore me, but they didn't do anything to make me feel welcome." I complained that I was the only Black woman in the entire group.

"Look—you joined an all-white group because you wanted a partner. So don't tell me about discrimination. You were there because you wanted to meet an attractive white woman. Now, things are different at GPW. The snobbiest women have left the group. Everybody's much more welcoming. You need to come back and find yourself a partner, Carol. You need a life."

It wasn't as if I hadn't tried to find a partner. I occasionally wandered downtown to go to the only two women's bars in Boston, Somewhere and The Saints. I made few friends there because I was neither a barfly nor an alcoholic. I couldn't dance and thought the bars were much too loud. Meeting a suitable partner at the bars was out of the question.

Also, I was a Jew and wanted a Jewish partner. As I scouted the bar crowd, it seemed that few Jewish singles hung out in bars. The women in the bars were also mostly white and did not go out of their way to meet the Black women there. I felt like an intruder even when I went to the bars with white friends.

However, I knew Tina was right. My only hope of avoiding a life of loneliness was to rejoin GPW. I'd left the group in a huff because of the way they tried to exclude women whom they thought weren't white collar professionals. That thought made me unhappy. I was relieved that Tina was taking over my social life and hoped that I'd meet her handpicked "suitable lesbians."

Although I was very shy about attending social gatherings of any kind, I told her I would go to the next meeting despite my misgivings. Tina and I together would attend the September meeting the next night.

The gathering was held in a member's apartment between Beacon Hill and my place. I reached the address—a beautiful brick townhouse with black shutters and a door knocker. The door was wide open. The living room was filled with lesbians of every description (except Black women), chattering, drinking, and laughing.

Most of the women seemed engaged in conversation. They appeared to be a very lively group. The living room was noisy, and there were outbursts of laughter now and then that punctuated the din. I spotted a few souls who were by themselves and clutching their drinks for lack of anything better to do. I decided that I would target them to see if I could start a conversation. Then I thought better of it. What did I have to offer? I wasn't a bona fide "professional woman." I was a graduate student who had years of being so ahead of me.

What were my other deficits that might make me less than desirable to GPW members, even to the loners? It occurred to me that being Black in such a white group wasn't a plus. However, most of my life I had been the only Black person present at work or at social gatherings of any kind. I was used to being "The First" or "The Only." When I became a Jew, I thought I was the first or the only Black Jew because I knew no other Black Jews except for the entertainer Sammy Davis Jr. Perhaps a white Jewish partner might accept me as "a different kind of Jew" and would be attracted to me because of my complexity.

I was thought to be peculiar by many Black people. I had only one Black friend, and she was in Philadelphia. Black lesbians tended to be Christian and didn't tolerate my having gone over to "the enemy, trying to be white."

Another strike against me was that I was attracted to white women only. I thought that white women would understand me because I had led a white life since high school. All my high school friends were white, and they were very accepting of me, especially if they were Jewish. All my college friends were white. Once I entered adulthood, I purposely sought out white friends. Why this passion for associating with whites? It was because they were more powerful than Black people. My Black family had raised me to be wary of Black people and to align myself with powerful white people as much as possible although I was the granddaughter of a former slave. How screwed up was that? Nevertheless, I listened to my parents and followed their dictates.

Additionally, I was five feet three inches tall and weighed 160 pounds at the time—decidedly more than I should have weighed. I never was one to dress up, much preferring old jeans, sneakers, and ordinary sweaters. Because of my appearance, I knew some people would reject me out of hand. Lastly, I had been clinically depressed since I was four years old—the age of my first serious suicide attempt.

After this uninviting assessment of myself, I jumped up from my chair and decided to leave the meeting before the guest speaker began her presentation about her professional career. However, once I was in the foyer, who should appear but Tina, surrounded by her devoted entourage of dependent lesbians. When she saw that I was about to depart, she quickly took my arm and turned me around.

"Carol! Where are you going? You're not leaving already!" She broke away from her little coterie so she would not be overheard.

"Look around you, Carol. You're seeing interesting professional women. And I've spotted two sexy Jewish women to whom I'll introduce you later. Now you just stay put, my dear. Trust me."

The hostess announced that the meeting was about to begin. Members ended their conversations and focused on her. After brief opening remarks, she introduced the night's speaker, Pat (no last name given lest someone out her), a manager of a computer hardware company somewhere in the suburbs. I was bored to death listening to her ramble on, so I began checking out the other women in the room. My judgment: no prospects.

When Pat finished, our hostess reappeared and reminded members about the date and location of next month's meeting, during which they would "hear from another successful woman."

Once announcements were finished, I thought I absolutely could not stand another minute in that apartment. I made some excuse to Tina that I had to study and rushed out of the building.

After a month had passed, it was time for the October GPW meeting. Since I had a much better idea of what the group was about and what kind of people belonged, I decided to attend my second meeting. Tina was busy with a portrait commission. Nevertheless, I decided to go alone.

On my way there, I had thought about my criteria for my ideal woman. I sought a white woman who was attractive, looked "straight," and was well educated, highly presentable, warm, caring, and very loving.

She would enjoy museums, classical music, and good food and wine and would love intense conversations about politics. She would be a fellow grad student or a professional woman. She would be Jewish and, although wondering why I chose Judaism, would be happy to be with another woman in the tribe. Having been in therapy herself, she would understand my mental illness. Frankly, I felt myself totally unworthy of such a prize.

Doing a quiet search of faces in the room, I did not see any prospects. Some women smiled at me and nodded hello. I did not know whether that kind of hello meant that I was supposed to walk across the room and strike up a conversation. Or perhaps it meant I was to wait in place and see what came from that. Fortunately, the meeting was about to start. Members were attempting to get out of the way as quickly as possible.

The evening's hostess moved to the front of the room and began to speak. She launched into the business part of the meeting by introducing the evening's guest speaker—a woman who also was a GPW member I'd never noticed before.

"Our guest speaker this evening is Cicely Stetson. She is a longtime resident of Boston. Professionally, she is the vice president for human resources at the Bank of Boston. This is quite an achievement because there are very few women in this country who have attained that level of power in a major bank." Then she signaled for Cicely to come to the front of the room.

My immediate impression of Cicely was that she didn't fit my mental description of a banker. I had pictured a woman dressed in a drab gray skirt suit who herself was drab. Instead, Cicely was very attractive. She wore a navy-blue blazer with gold buttons, a cream-colored shirt, a blue paisley silk kerchief tied around her neck, navy-blue slacks, and navy-blue leather shoes that had a slim gold horizontal band atop a red-and-green-striped cloth band. From the photos I'd seen in *Esquire*, I knew that she was wearing very expensive Gucci loafers. Her only adornments were a pair of small gold earrings and a watch. I assessed her appearance as quiet, good taste. I also noted that she had blonde curly hair that was very well coifed, a face that radiated warmth and ease, and beautiful blue eyes. She appeared to be in her mid-thirties—the average age of most GPW members.

After clearing her throat, she began her presentation. I thought she was a handsome woman who didn't look Jewish (but neither did I). My guess that she was probably a WASP because she had ramrod straight posture that framed her medium height.

She didn't begin her presentation with a joke. Instead, she launched into her speech with great seriousness and did not waste a word. I was favorably disposed toward her from the outset of her talk.

As she discussed her rise to prominence, Cicely spoke about how difficult it was to be in an all-male working environment. She discussed her efforts to hire more minorities and women to fill professional job openings at the bank, particularly if the recruits were graduates who'd trained in elite business schools. It occurred to me that her performance over the years must have been stellar and that she had benefited from excellent mentoring.

As I listened to her presentation, I thought hers was the best presentation I'd heard from any of the GPW speakers. Usually the speakers, no matter how well rehearsed, bored me. Now that Cicely was giving such an excellent presentation, I tuned in. Although I had zero interest in pursuing a career in banking, I was so impressed by her presentation that I decided to thank her for sharing her story with us.

At the end of her talk, I pushed my way through the crowd to reach the place where she stood. However, I saw that there were several others ahead of me who were shaking her hand, asking questions, or just making social small talk.

When it was finally my turn to speak with her, I had to force my right arm to extend itself and thereby entice her to take my sweaty hand. My entire body was trembling as I managed to get my act together enough to say some simple words to her: "Thank you for your talk. It was very interesting, and I enjoyed it." Phew! I did it!

Cicely very firmly and graciously took my hand in hers and shook it. As she did so, she smiled and told me that she was glad that I'd enjoyed it. Then she relaxed her grip and asked me if I wanted something to drink—that she was headed for the table filled with various bottles of wine. For some reason, although I wanted to say "yes, I'll join you," I replied that I was fine.

She then turned away from me, walked to the table where she was greeted by more members, and poured two glasses of wine—one for another member and one for herself. When both had finished, they put their glasses on a small mahogany table, thanked the hostess, and left the gathering.

I had no intention of staying any longer to stand around and have uncomfortably meaningless conversations with those who continued to stay. I made my way toward the host, thanked her for her hospitality, and left the building to go back to my apartment.

As I walked up Beacon Street, I wondered if the woman with whom she'd left the meeting was Cicely's partner. What I'd noticed at the meeting was that Cicely seemed to have quite a few friends and this woman was another friend of hers. In any case, although I found Cicely very interesting, I assumed that I would never be in her social circle. I was twenty-nine, awkward, and, in my estimation, highly undesirable.

About a week after the October GPW meeting, my phone rang late one afternoon. When I answered it, I heard the voice of my friend Marilyn. I particularly liked her because she always had good ideas about activities that were fun to do together.

After our pleasantries, Marilyn announced that she was having a party for women only at her home this coming Saturday night and wanted me to come. I readily accepted her invitation.

"But you must come alone," she said.

"Why? I'd like to bring a friend from school who's on my gaydar."

However, Marilyn was adamant that I bring no date. "Just bring yourself. The party starts at seven. Can't wait to see you!"

Saturday evening arrived very quickly—in fact, so quickly that I hadn't had much time to worry about it beforehand. However, the closer it came to being seven o'clock, the more nervous I became. After I checked the mirror to make sure that I was presentably dressed for a change and that my long Afro was patted perfectly in place, I left my apartment and headed for Marilyn's building.

I rang her bell with trepidation, and she buzzed me in. As I entered her small vestibule, Marilyn quickly gave me an approving glance, warmly hugged me, and ushered me inside. As we entered her living room, I saw that it was packed with women who appeared to be in their late twenties or early thirties. All were white—not that there being no other Black women presented a problem to me. How I longed to be included.

I snaked my way through the crowd and sat down on the loveseat. Another woman already was seated there. I said hello, and we exchanged some small talk about the weather and where we lived. Shortly afterward, she stood up, excused herself, and left the sofa to sit on the floor with a few other women.

I wasn't alone for more than a minute before Marilyn joined me. After quickly patting my shoulder, she smiled and asked me how I was. I responded that I was enjoying my studies and that school had just enough crazy people to make me feel at home. She laughed heartily at that because she thought I was joking. I wasn't. She knew nothing about my mental health problems, and that was fine with me. Fearing that she might have taken my remark seriously, I quickly changed the subject to discussing her latest office stories.

While Marilyn and I were catching up, her doorbell rang again. When she opened the door, who should walk in but Cicely! At her side was the woman I'd seen her leave with at the end of her GPW presentation. Seeing them together, I realized that they were more than friends; they were a couple.

As they entered the living room filled with women's bodies, I took time to evaluate Cicely's partner. She looked a few years older than Cicely. She was very well dressed, her blonde hair was perfectly coifed, and she seemed quite elegant but aloof as she circled the room looking for a place to sit. Cicely appeared to be very relaxed and smiled a great deal as she chatted with Marilyn. I wondered why Marilyn had allowed her to bring a date.

I began eavesdropping on conversations, especially the ones that seemed to have the most interesting gossip about women with whom I was acquainted. I found it amusing to hear the hot skinny about who was sleeping with whom, who had found a new job, and so on.

In the meantime, someone else sat down beside me. I turned my head and was very surprised to see it was Cicely.

"Hello. I'm Cicely."

"Hi. I'm Carol. I'm a friend of Marilyn's. I live up the street. By the way, I was at GPW the night you gave your talk about your career, and I enjoyed your presentation."

This time when I was talking with her, I was a little more relaxed, but I kept looking at her face for signs of boredom. There were none. In fact, she looked as though she were going to remark about what I'd just said.

"Thank you." She was very gracious in accepting my praise, although I could tell by her tone of voice that she didn't remember me. Perhaps that was a good thing. "Well, you know what I do. What do you do?" She turned to face me while awaiting my answer. As I looked into her eyes, I saw that she seemed genuinely interested in what I did for a living. How would I explain to her that I didn't have a job anywhere?

"I'm a graduate student." Here I was talking with a very successful corporate woman about my station in life as a lowly student. However, instead of looking bored, she looked more closely at me.

"Where are you doing your work and what's your research area?"

It was one thing to ask me where I was studying, but people rarely asked me about my research. I was very surprised that she was interested.

"At MIT in political science. This is my first semester in the doctoral program. My research to date has centered on Third World political economy." I checked to see if she was bored. No signs of boredom yet.

She smiled again and mentioned that she was very interested in politics. She told me that she'd been working for the passage of the Equal Rights Amendment. I was impressed since I hardly took her to be an activist. Although I'd declared myself a feminist, I wasn't an activist. In Philadelphia I had belonged to a consciousness-raising group called Radical Lesbians. We talked about being radical, but week after week we just griped.

Cicely was a buttoned-down corporate activist. Of course, I shouldn't have been surprised because during her GPW presentation she'd spent a considerable amount of time discussing the need for more people from minority groups and women to enter banking as a career and her persistent recruitment efforts to attract such people to her bank. She had seemed very dedicated to diversifying her corporate environment. That she cared about women's rights was icing on the cake as far as I was concerned.

"Why are you interested in politics?" Her tone of voice signaled to me that she really wanted an honest answer to her question. I had to resist making a self-effacing joke to brush her off.

I thoughtfully considered her question before I answered. Just how much did she want to hear about my background? I didn't want to scare her off by telling her about my previous jobs in Philadelphia and Cambridge.

"I've worked in political settings and government. When I finish my degree, I hope to start my own consulting firm or return to a former organization at which I have worked, Abt Associates in Cambridge. If I return to Abt, I'll be a senior researcher."

She frowned slightly before asking her next question. "If you're planning for a future in consulting, why aren't you at the 'B' school [meaning Harvard Business School]? It would be useful for you to have a degree in business."

I was horrified at the thought of being at the "B" school. First, I didn't think I was intelligent enough to have matriculated there. Second, the school struck me as populated by hordes of men focused on becoming millionaires as quickly as possible, ethics be damned. Third, I was becoming too politically radical in grad school to have survived the "B" school's take on capitalism.

"No, not really. I'm interested in business, but I enjoy the work that I'm doing right now. My classes are very stimulating. They're small seminars taught by well-known professors. My cohort has only thirteen first-year students." Now it was my turn to ask a question. "Cicely, how do you know Marilyn?"

I was very curious about their connection since Marilyn had never mentioned Cicely or invited her to be with us. Perhaps Cicely was an ex-lover of Marilyn's or had met Marilyn at GPW. Instead of answering my question in a way that would have ended the mystery for me, Cicely smiled and said, "Oh, we've been friends for years. I forget how we met." I noticed that when she said that there was a distinctive twinkle in her eyes. I found that charming. If she was a friend of Marilyn's, she must be a fun-lover. Yet it was strange that neither Tina nor Marilyn had ever mentioned a woman named Cicely.

"She's terrific and loves to have a good time. She told me that the two of you had visited the bars together," said Cicely with a smile. Then she peered over my shoulder as though she were looking for someone. Perhaps she was looking for her partner.

She turned to me and asked, "Do you know any of these people?"

"Yes. I've seen some of them at GPW. Marilyn knows tons of interesting people."

Cicely nodded in agreement. I wanted to ask about her partner, but just as I was about to do that, Marilyn announced that dinner was served. Cicely and I walked together to the table. Before she served herself, she consulted her partner, who shook her head no. I thought that meant she didn't want anything. Her partner sat with her hands clasped, deep in conversation with another woman. As I began to serve myself, Cicely drifted away to talk with someone else. I returned to my seat on the sofa and ate dinner. Then, for lack of anything better to do, I decided to help Marilyn with the dishes.

I gathered several empty plates and went through the swinging door into her kitchen. Marilyn thanked me and showed me where the dishes should go. Then she moved toward me and began whispering excitedly.

"Somebody out there likes you, Carol." She began to giggle like a teenage girl who had just seen the football player she had a crush on.

"Who?" I asked. Perhaps the woman who had sat next to me at first but said little. Maybe she was taking stock of me and wanted to watch me interact with other guests. No matter how hard I tried, I couldn't imagine who this interested someone could be.

Then Marilyn laughed and exclaimed, "It's Cicely!"

"Cicely?" I was stunned by this revelation. I'd never thought that Cicely, of all people, would have liked me enough to mention me to Marilyn.

"You're kidding! Wait a minute—Do you mean she likes me as a friend? She came here with her partner."

Marilyn's smile faded and she became serious.

"Oh, don't worry about that. It's a long story. Too boring for now." She waved her hand as if swatting my question away. "Just take my word for it."

How could Cicely be interested in me? We had spoken for less than fifteen minutes. And when did she tell Marilyn that she had any interest in me?

Marilyn continued, "She wants to know if she can call you. Can I give her your number?"

I hesitated for only a few seconds before I answered Marilyn's question. "Well, okay. Tell her she can call me the week after next." I was excited but puzzled. Why would Cicely want to be friends with me? Perhaps she loved politics more than I'd assumed.

But, hesitancy aside, I was thrilled that Cicely liked me enough to want to call me. I thought she'd be an interesting friend. She was interested in my work. Also, I welcomed friendships with powerful people, especially if they were lesbians.

I tried not to grin, but I was elated. This important woman wanted *my* phone number. I thought that I must have been dreaming or had too much wine to think straight.

After I thanked Marilyn for the news, I went back into the living room. To my great dismay, I saw Cicely and her partner standing up, about to leave the party. They waited until Marilyn came out of the kitchen, said they had to leave a little early, and thanked her—or at least, Cicely thanked her. With that, she and her partner left and went into the night.

I was disappointed that I didn't get another chance to talk with Cicely and was sorry that I wouldn't hear from her for a week. She might change her mind about pursuing a friendship with me. She might entirely forget about me.

In the meantime, I had to stop dreaming about The One. I had faith that she existed somewhere. Perhaps I'd missed my golden opportunity to meet her. I hoped that wasn't the case. Had I been so blind as to overlook her during my quest and not have seen the forest for the trees? But then again . . .

Here's a teaser for the full memoir: Cicely became my life partner. We remain together to this day in our senior years.

Chapter 11

Leslie Feinberg's Complex
Jewish Lesbian Feminism

MARLA BRETTSCHNEIDER

Introduction

Leslie Feinberg was a political activist and thinker who described herself[1] as an "anti-racist white, working-class, secular Jewish, transgender, lesbian, female, revolutionary communist."[2] For Feinberg, these multiple aspects of her identity related inherently to her political work in justice movements. Due to antisemitism on the left, including in lesbian and queer feminist communities, activists and scholars often overlook Feinberg's Jewishness.[3] Lack of attention to Jewish matters, as well as to Christian privilege and Christian hegemony, are perilous and often deadly.[4] While we in the US are getting better at recognizing white, straight, cisgender, class, and certain other forms of privilege, we have hardly begun the journey to explore Christian privilege. Feinberg's revolutionary politics addresses that lacuna, among others, in social justice movements. By centering Feinberg's Jewishness, we can interrupt the repetition of ignoring Jewishness and better understand Feinberg and these movements. Feinberg's experiences reflect the ways that race, gender, culture, and class and discrimination based on these identity groupings are mutually constituted. In other words, each one of these identities helps to create and shape each of the others. In examining the ways in which Feinberg's multifaceted, mutually constituted identities and politics are also simultaneously co-constructed with her Jewish historical context, we can note that in all of Feinberg's radicalness, she was also a relatively normative US Jew; in other words, within the context of Ashkenazi Jewish history and contemporary US Jewish demographic studies, she was relatively conventional in many ways—including in some aspects of her life that made her stand out.

For example, Feinberg stood out in her relationship to gender and sexuality. In the late nineteenth and early twentieth centuries, gender nonconforming people and those whose sexuality was anything other than simply heterosexual were often called "inverts." Ashkenazi Jews, in particular, have long been hated for what was considered their inversion, for purportedly turning the world upside down. These Jews, by maintaining gender norms markedly different from those of their Christian neighbors, were problematically disorienting to the dominant groups in the various regions they lived in Christendom. In this regard, Feinberg is not an isolated example. At the same time, the ways in which Feinberg transformed "inversion" into multilayered, intersectional justice politics situated her as exceptional. This transformation was as deeply Jewish as it was exceptional. As will be demonstrated below, Feinberg continued the Jewish tradition of inverting and transforming the status quo. Thus, ironically, while Feinberg pushed boundaries and was a gender outlaw in many extraordinary ways, she was also a relatively normative (i.e., typical) US Jew, both empirically and in terms of her values.

This chapter begins with a brief biographical sketch, after which readers will find sections based on each of five well-known and primary vectors of Feinberg's justice politics: lesbian feminism, anti-racism, class-based organizing, trans activism, and multicultural coalition work. These politics themselves are co-constructed, and they informed Feinberg's own mutually constitutive identities, which in turn added to her political analysis as they continued to develop. For Feinberg, Jewishness, Jewish history, and her Jewish cultural and political associations were central to each of these vectors. Accordingly, in each section I examine a particular vector, co-constituted with the other four, and place these co-constructed aspects of her identity and politics into a Jewish context. Readers may realize that there are Jews who are women, lesbians, white, working class, and trans, as a matter of complex identity demographics. Here I examine the centrality of Feinberg's multilayered intersectional politics (principally lesbian, feminist, class-based, critical race, trans, and multicommunity coalition activism) within the history of US Jewish experience. We find that, for Feinberg, Jewish history and her Jewish cultural and political associations simultaneously inform the other aspects of her justice politics.

Feinberg's Biography

Born in Missouri in 1947, directly following the Nazi Holocaust, and raised in working-class Buffalo during the 1950s and 1960s, Leslie Feinberg was a gifted activist, organizer, speaker, and writer. She is probably most often remembered in lesbian feminist communities for her thoughtful exploration of transgender identity. However, Feinberg remained committed throughout her life to fighting political oppression in many co-created forms.

Feinberg participated in numerous feminist, labor, anti-antisemitic, anti-racist, queer, and anti-war actions from the late 1960s on. Feinberg developed her talents, analysis, and leadership skills as she contributed to organizing these actions. In this work, she demonstrated nuanced sensitivities that brought people into her sphere. Although she faced intense bigotry,[5] Feinberg became a leader from an early age. Feinberg joined the Workers World Party in the late 1960s. During the Boston busing riots of 1974, she organized a group of "lesbian-identified people" to lead an all-night "paste-up" covering graffiti that used racial epithets. Feinberg participated in a national tour to raise AIDS awareness, worked to rout Klan members on Martin Luther King Jr. Day in Atlanta, and organized against anti-abortion activists in Buffalo. Because her Jewish political commitments included advocating for Palestinian rights and dignity, she chose to donate the proceeds from the Hebrew translation of *Stone Butch Blues* to an organization benefiting gay Palestinian women.[6]

Even a partial list of the justice issues for which Feinberg fought reflects the broader ways one needs to understand Feinberg, her Jewishness, and her legacy. She also worked on all of these issues in and through her writing. After publishing two pamphlets (in 1980 and 1992), Feinberg gained widespread recognition in 1993 with *Stone Butch Blues*, a semi-autobiographical work of fiction about a Jewish trans person growing up in working-class Buffalo in the 1960s. Feinberg authored another work of fiction, *Drag King Dreams*, and two nonfiction books, *Transgender Warriors: Making History* and *Trans Liberation: Beyond Pink and Blue*. Feinberg also published a collection of twenty-five journalistic articles, *Rainbow Solidarity in Defense of Cuba*, as well as a series of web articles exploring LGBTQ history for the Workers World Party called *Lavender & Red*.

Feinberg's Lesbian Feminism

Feinberg was an Ashkenazi Jewish, gender nonconforming lesbian raised in a working-class family in Buffalo in the 1950s and 1960s. Feinberg's lesbian feminist politics emerged specifically as anti-racist and as trans revolutionary communist in a Jewish context.[7] From her early days, Feinberg's thinking and activism included opposing patriarchy.[8] While many Jewish activists of her era were drawn to feminism, Feinberg did not initially move into this path in community with other Jewish feminists, probably largely because she lived outside major urban centers with sizeable Jewish populations. Feinberg engaged in lesbian feminist activism with other Jews only when she was able to widen her circles in the 1970s and 1980s.[9] Seeking empowerment both within Jewish circles and in the wider US culture, Jewish women, lesbians, bisexuals, and gender benders increasingly organized as feminists to address the sexism, heterosexism, and cisgendered hegemony they encountered.[10] Of course, there have long been Jewish and other gender outlaws, and the Jewish feminist and lesbian feminist movements in the US came into their own by the early 1980s as part of the larger feminist and lesbian feminist movements. By the time of the publication of Feinberg's first book in 1993, Jewish feminist and lesbian feminist activism and writing had reached a level of coherence within which her work could be embraced on a national level.[11]

In this time frame, many Jewish lesbians created a self-conscious political and cultural identity as Jewish lesbian feminists. Like Feinberg, many Jewish feminists, particularly Jewish lesbian feminists, struggled with being public regarding their Jewish identity and often did not engage politically as Jews, especially not at the start of their activism. An assimilationist assumption and the overt and underlying antisemitic pressure were too great.[12] As Jewish feminism and trans and lesbian feminisms grew, more space emerged for a range of self-identified Jewish feminists and lesbian and trans feminists, and they continued actively creating that space. We can see this shift in Feinberg's work.

In her 1993 *Stone Butch Blues*, the protagonist, Jess Goldberg, is clearly Jewish. However, beyond familial and community relations of her childhood, Jewish ties are largely absent from the narrative. In her 2006 *Drag King Dreams*, Feinberg's central character, Max Rabinowitz, is more reflective about Jewishness, has various Jewishly related engagements, and regularly relies on a Jewish friend, Hesh. While the cis, straight, male Hesh is outside of Max's tight-knit group of coworkers and activists, exchanges with this character provide avenues for many of the explorations of Max's Jewishness. Feinberg also makes sure to include other Jewish characters, such as Estelle and Vickie, who are queerly gendered and sexed and part of Max's political community. Feinberg is more Jewishly grounded in her second novel and more in touch with Jewish diversity.[13]

By 1993, when Feinberg published *Stone Butch Blues*, Jewish lesbian feminism had gained significant traction in Jewish, Jewish feminist, and broader lesbian and feminist circles. Evelyn Torton Beck's groundbreaking *Nice Jewish Girls* set the stage for this in 1982. In 1986, Elly Bulkin, Barbara Smith, and Minnie Bruce Pratt (who later became Feinberg's life partner) published *Yours in Struggle*. These three lesbian feminist thinkers and activists—one white and Jewish, one Black and non-Jewish, and one white and non-Jewish—took on difficult aspects of racism and antisemitism in the lesbian and feminist communities as well as in wider US culture. Also in 1986, Melanie Kaye/Kantrowitz and Irena Klepfisz published a special double issue of the journal *Sinister Wisdom* entitled *The Tribe of Dina*. Here, Kaye/Kantrowitz and Klepfisz brought together Jewish lesbians and feminists to address multilayered diversity issues among Jews and in the US more broadly. Feinberg's 1993 Jewish, lesbian, feminist, anti-racist, working-class heroine fit well within this burgeoning Jewish feminist and lesbian feminist milieu even as Feinberg's novel set a new course by centering trans experience and issues.

Feinberg and her fictional protagonists Jess and Max were cultural, secular Jews, as are most Jews in the US.[14] In an era when Jews are increasingly portrayed by feminists and the left in the US as right-wing, it is important to understand Feinberg's lesbian feminist commitments as relatively aligned with Jewish (US) American norms. Like the 73 percent of US Jews who note that remembering the Nazi Holocaust is important to their understanding of Jewish identity, Feinberg was motivated by a post-Holocaust Jewish sensibility and lesbian feminist, anti-fascist politics.[15] The complex leftist activism to which Feinberg's lesbian feminism led her is also generally in line with the values of most Jews, who consider leading an ethical life essential to their Jewishness, and specifically with those of the slightly smaller majority who say that their Jewish identity requires working for justice and equality.[16] While the US Jewish community is diverse and dynamic in many ways, lesbian feminist Leslie Feinberg's political values were rather normatively Jewish.

Feinberg, Whiteness, and Anti-Racism

Like most Jews in the US in her time, Feinberg was apparently Ashkenazi. Currently, US taxonomies (especially from thinkers on the left) usually identify such Jews as white. Feinberg self-identified Jewishly and also racially as an "anti-racist white." Feinberg, like many Jews in the US, set anti-racism at the center of her work.[17] A Jewish setting for Feinberg helps us to see that race in the US is not a static assignation. Feinberg's access to white privilege changed over her lifetime. In order to understand Feinberg's socially constructed whiteness as an identity co-created through her anti-racism as a politics, let us look at the changing racial status of US Jews in the mid-twentieth century.

Historically, many Jews in the US were considered non-white, while some were not quite white or, at most, precariously white.[18] The transition of some Jews toward whiteness in general and to a less precarious whiteness is inextricably bound up in the genocide and imperialism at the core of the creation of the nation-states of modern Europe in the imperial age of the Atlantic slave trade and colonization. Since the fifteenth century, some of the first Jews in what we now call the US came here as enslaved persons from western Africa.[19] Others came from Portugal and Spain in flight from the Spanish Inquisition.[20] Feinberg's family came to the US as part of a later eastern and central European immigration.[21]

Both Sephardi and Ashkenazi Jews were considered white in certain arenas in the US but not in others. Until the mid-twentieth century, even Ashkenazi, Euro-heritage Jews (whose skin was generally lighter than that of Jews from other regions) generally fell outside of the classifications of whiteness as they emerged in common US (Christian) typologies. Feinberg was born just after World War II and the Nazi Holocaust. Seeking to distance themselves from the recently squelched Nazi threat, dominant US Christian whites sought to move US antisemitism underground. In this moment, they began a racial reassignment of European-heritage Jews in the United States from an initial designation as non-white to not quite white, and then to a new status as potential honorary whites.[22] By adulthood, Feinberg was able to access white privilege a bit more consistently.

Despite the actual diversity of US Jews in terms of race and ethnicity, by the 1970s, European-heritage Jews were increasingly considered white, particularly in urban areas of the US Northeast, where Feinberg lived. As Feinberg's family experience demonstrates, however, this new privileged status was neither simple nor guaranteed.

Whiteness in the US has been understood historically within a Christian framework.[23] Protecting elite Christian hegemony, this recent racial reassignment remains dependent on assimilation to Christian, white, middle-class norms, including mutually constitutive characteristics, such as heterosexuality, gender normativity, and mainstream or right-wing political affiliation.[24] When Jews defy normative expectations, this new status and access to privilege is easily withheld, as we saw during McCarthyism. Emerging on the heels of the Holocaust, the Red Scare targeted Jews disproportionately, both in the US and transnationally.[25] During the Red Scare, Feinberg, as a gender nonconforming Jew, brought a threatening degree of attention to her working-class family, whose economic situation was already precarious.[26]

Thus, the racial reassignment remained conditional but nonetheless significant; it provided conditional, honorary access to white privilege within a system of white Christian supremacy. Many European-heritage Jews, like Feinberg, take responsibility for this privilege both by acknowledging it explicitly and by being active in anti-racism work. For Feinberg, using the modifier *anti-racist* to qualify her whiteness was an essential part of how she held herself accountable for the shifting white privilege provided by a given historical moment. Feinberg's use of this qualifier for her identity as white is an explicitly political move. Self-identifying as Jewish puts her whiteness into a specific historical and political frame within US white Christian hegemony. At the same time, her specifying "anti-racist white" as her racial identification is also an act of resistance to hegemonic whiteness. This act interrupts a reiterative performance of whiteness that helps to make and keep whiteness "naturally" normative in a system of white supremacy.[27]

Feinberg, Class, and Labor Activism

Feinberg was raised working class. Noting how aspects of identity are co-constructed with justice politics, we can examine ways in which Feinberg's Jewishness and Jewish-inspired politics brought her into class-based work. Feinberg's Jewish identity made her a passionate participant in Palestinian justice activism,[28] and it was at a demonstration for Palestinian rights and self-determination that a young Feinberg first encountered the Workers World Party. Feinberg then joined the Buffalo branch of this party and went on to national communist and labor organizing.[29] Feinberg's Jewish class identity continued to develop in tandem with her politics. As part of her ongoing labor commitment, Feinberg continued to engage in Palestinian justice work and in activism seeking to end race-based forms of oppression. She worked in anti-racism both to end oppression generally and as a way to take responsibility for some aspects of a newly acquired access to white privilege. Additionally, Feinberg spent the rest of her life working against antisemitism and insisting that labor organizing also include anti-racist, anti-patriarchal, anti-homophobic, and anti-transphobic agendas. Like masses of other Jews, she relied on her post-Holocaust experience and studies of the Holocaust to hone the anti-fascism that was at the core of her communism and labor organizing.[30]

By maintaining an anti-racist focus in labor organizing and activism, Feinberg was challenging a major pillar of white supremacy. Key to the invention of whiteness in the US was a move to cleave the underclass by severing working-class European immigrants from working-class (US) Americans of African heritage.[31] As some white-designated minority ethnic groups grew financially stable, they eschewed both cross-racial and cross-class alliances. Understanding the classed nature of the creation of whiteness is important. It is also instructive to explore the ways in which, as a Jew, Feinberg stands outside of the important narratives that progressive historians have generally developed linking race and class.

As we know, Feinberg was a working-class, European-heritage Jew who engaged in labor organizing.[32] This situates her squarely within the mainstream of twentieth-century US Jewish history. Along with Mizrahi, Sephardi, and western-European-heritage Jews, central- and eastern-European-heritage Jews have long been at the forefront of communist, socialist, anarchist, and general labor organizing in the US.[33] Their engagement in these movements was often also inextricably connected with Jewish anti-racism work.[34]

Additionally, Jewish working-class activists were familiar with the need to create their own organizations because the English-speaking, white, Christian, working-class organizations in the US generally excluded Jews. (Feinberg would note here that it generally excluded queers as well.)[35] US-born, white, Christian labor activists were suspicious of new immigrant populations as potentially undercutting wages for US-born, white, Christian men; these suspicions continue today. Thus, Jews in the US had a history of organizing their own groups and working closely with other labor activists, socialists, communists, anarchists, and trade unionists. This multilayered Jewish vision and set of organizing skills can be seen in Feinberg's life, work, and labor organizing.[36]

Placing Feinberg in this Jewish context demonstrates the need for new narratives about the co-construction of race, class, white Christian supremacy, and investment in capitalism. Karen Brodkin identifies the aforementioned mid- to late-twentieth-century racial reassignment of numerous US Jews from non-white to honorary white as bound with a class transformation. Many US Jews at this time were also moving from the poor and working classes to the middle class.[37] However, US Jews defy demographic trends and academic expectations that increasing wealth and white status are coterminous with alliance with capitalist white Christian supremacy. Instead, even with these demographic shifts, US Jews generally continued their work as labor organizers and participated in the civil rights and anti-racist movements in numbers disproportionate to other groups except US Black Americans.[38] The trajectory of Feinberg's participation in the Workers World Party from the early 1970s until her death in 2014 remained in line with this US Jewish investment in labor, socialist, communist, and anarchist organizing even as many Jews moved into the middle class and simultaneously came to self-identify as white, as Feinberg did.[39]

Trans, Queers, and Gender Outlaws

Central to Feinberg's lesbian feminist, anti-racist labor organizing is her work as a lesbian, feminist trans activist. Feinberg's trans political analysis and activism grew out of her experiences as gender nonconforming, and, at the same time, that analysis and organizing experience honed her self-awareness. Throughout her life, Feinberg insisted on fighting for a variety of oppressed groups and individuals and simultaneously exploring what gender and sexuality mean to individuals in a given setting.[40] Feinberg inspired a younger generation of trans people, such as Jewish activist Sasha Goldberg,[41] who in the early 1990s articulated that being trans and genderqueer means pushing beyond not only the cisnormative gender binaries of male and female but also the growing tendency in trans activism to operate in a new trans/cis binary.[42]

It is important to bring Feinberg's Jewish history into understanding her challenge to binary gender orthodoxies. Feinberg came from European Jewish stock, which has long confounded normative Western sexual and gender binaries. In European Christiandom for most of the modern era, Ashkenazi Jews were considered "queer."[43]

In the 1990s, Feinberg both helped to create and was supported by a discourse and a movement for people to understand themselves and each other as transgender. This iteration of the movement sought to replace the often medically imposed and restraining concept "transsexual" with the more self-defined and malleable concept "transgender" commonly found in queer theory and activism today.[44] Feinberg eschewed the constant requirement to indicate her "sex" on official documents, and her objections extended to the idea of indicating "transgender" in the same way, as a box to check off.[45] Feinberg sought not simply to move from F to M, or from either M or F to T, but instead to open up spaces to enhance the capacity of people to express their own concepts of gender with maximal freedom.[46]

While this seems new on the anti-binary gender axis in the US, it is not so new for European Jews and the traditions from which Feinberg comes. The idea of a gender binary is not as clear in Jewish history as it is in modern Western Christiandom.[47] Even within the binary, European Jewish communities did not operate with a hegemonic assumption that men should be physically strong, leaders in business, and the primary financial support for their families. Historically, most Ashkenazi European Jews were extremely poor and sometimes illiterate, but the elite aspiration for Jewish men was to be scholars of ancient Jewish texts. To allow men to engage in scholarly pursuits, Jewish women frequently engaged in business, ran their family finances, and sustained their families economically. Significantly, this meant that both men and women in Jewish communities tended to be more literate than the non-Jews in their surrounding communities. Many Jewish women needed math, business skills, and writing. Because they interfaced with the surrounding communities regularly, they often needed multilingual fluency.

These activities and skills defied Christian European gender norms. Thus, among the many reasons Christian Europeans hated Jews and considered them suspect was that Jews, as a community, were queerly gendered.[48] According to the binaries of modern Christiandom, Jewish women seemed mannish, and the men appeared feminized. Gender norms and heteronormativity co-construct each other—gender is created through heteronormativity, and heteronormativity is simultaneously created through gender norms. Thus, the inherently queer gender of European Ashkenazi Jews also rendered them suspect as sexual perverts and as a people who could not be counted on to uphold heterosexual norms.[49] Traditional Christian gendered and sexual binaries operated differently for Ashkenazi Jews. We find that Feinberg stands solidly among other US Jews, such as Kate Bornstein and Judith Butler, as well-known Jewish gender outlaws of their generation. This is also how Feinberg can identify as trans and lesbian and a woman in an identity group that pushes the borders of all three of those categories. Informed by her Jewish history, she insisted on self-defining as she pushed back against Western, Christian-dominant categories of gender and sexuality.

Solidarity, Ally, and Multicultural Organizing

This section explores Feinberg's self-identification through a multiplicity of politically salient characteristics along with her commitment to working in multicultural coalitions.[50] In fact, Feinberg's last project (unfinished as of her death but being completed by friends as of this writing) was developing a twentieth-anniversary edition of her first novel. Feinberg sought to create a free edition of the book with a slideshow, "This Is What Solidarity Looks Like." The slideshow focused on the campaign on behalf of the (trans) woman activist CeCe McDonald. McDonald was imprisoned for an act of self-defense when a white neo-Nazi attacked her.[51] In this endeavor, as in so much of her work, Feinberg demonstrated an exquisite capacity for multicultural solidarity and ally development. In her political thinking, organizing, and writing, she managed to bring together many multifaceted identity groups for deep work on joint political projects, and she often clarified a Jewish connection as she did so.[52] In this, she also falls clearly within a US Jewish norm.

Feinberg self-identified with multiple communities based on class, race, gender, culture, and sexuality.[53] This compound identity was a facet of her complex political vision, grounded in multiplicity and work building multicultural activist coalitions.[54] It is instructive to understand Feinberg's signature coalition style within a Jewish context.[55] Like Feinberg, most eastern European Jews were poor, and many acquired long years of working-class and political organizing experience.[56] Given anti-Jewish sentiment and extremism, as well as the segregation of European Jews into ghettos, Jewish communities developed complex, multinational networks and mutual aid organizations. They also brought this expertise with them as immigrants and refugees to the US. As a small minority in the US, Jews needed to bridge gaps between their own organizations and other justice movements. In a majoritarian system, such a small and marginalized minority, however well organized, cannot get far in its aspirations for self-protection and social transformation.[57]

Feinberg performed and mobilized this multicommunity coalitional orientation in concrete politics in her writing as well as in her activism. For example, in each of her novels, the primary Jewish character is situated in a complex web of diverse characters and activist initiatives based on race, culture, class, gender, and sexuality. Feinberg applies this method in her nonfiction works as well.[58] In *Transgender Warriors*, Feinberg does this through historical analysis, and in *Trans Liberation*, Feinberg brings in first-person contributions from a diverse set of contemporary activists. Using these methods, Feinberg makes use of her relatively privileged access to publishing to raise up the voices and experiences of other marginalized people without such privilege. In her writing projects,[59] Feinberg is also explicit about Jewish history and political insights as she weaves together analyses of numerous identity communities and movement politics.

Conclusion

Leslie Feinberg was a remarkable person who bequeathed a rich, innovative legacy to Jews and to all political activists and thinkers. While in many ways exceptional, she was also in many ways empirically normative within the Jewish culture of her time and place. That Feinberg and her commitments in justice politics are situated so Jewishly may not previously have been known to many of her allies and readers.

Radical thinking and activism addressing gender binaries was central as one of many axes in Feinberg's lifework. Placed within a Jewish historical context, Feinberg's radical engagement with antisemitism and her feminism, lesbian visions, trans development, anti-racism, and critical class consciousness reveal great internal cohesion. For Feinberg, these identities and areas of activism influenced each other, co-creating her multidimensionality as she purposefully centered her own identity while working in complex solidarity with others.

Notes

Thanks to Joelle Ruby Ryan, Esther Rothblum, Nina Katz, Alden Reed, Patrick Baga, Bethany Kaminsky, Marina Cardoso-Vianna-Vaz, Ben Mackillop, Jane Litman, and the anonymous reviewers. Brief versions of my work on Feinberg are published in Jane Litman and Jakob Hero-Shaw, *Liberating Gender for Jews and Allies: The Wisdom of Transkeit* (Newcastle upon Tyne, UK: Cambridge Scholars Publishing, 2022) and in *The Shalvi/Hyman Encyclopedia of Jewish Women*.

    1. Since Feinberg's passing, it has become common for trans people and allies to utilize third-person pronouns (they/their/theirs) to disrupt binary gender politics. In an attempt to honor Feinberg's personal and political choices during her life, in this article I will refer to Feinberg with feminine pronouns (she/her), primarily because this book is not an all-trans setting; in a 2006 interview, Feinberg explained her pronoun preferences, illustrating her awareness of numerous complex issues:

> For me, pronouns are always placed within context. I am female-bodied, I am a butch lesbian, a transgender lesbian—referring to me as "she/her" is appropriate, particularly in a non-trans setting in which referring to me as "he" would appear to resolve the social contradiction between my birth sex and my gender expression and render my transgender expression invisible. I like the gender-neutral pronoun "ze/hir" because it makes it impossible to hold on to gender/sex/sexuality assumptions about a person you're about to meet or you've just met. And in an all trans setting, referring to me as "he/him" honors my gender expression in the same way that referring to my sister drag queens as "she/her" does. (Jamie Tyroler, "Interview with Leslie Feinberg," *Camp Magazine* website, July 28, 2006, http://www.campkc.com/campkc-content.php?Page_ID=225 [site discontinued])

Shortly before her death, Feinberg and Pratt wrote, "Leslie preferred to use the pronouns she/zie and her/hir for hirself, but also said: 'I care which pronoun is used, but people have been respectful to me with the wrong pronoun and disrespectful with the right one. It matters whether someone is using the pronoun as a bigot, or if they are trying to demonstrate respect.'" Leslie Feinberg and Minnie Bruce Pratt, "Leslie Feinberg (1949–2014)," on Leslie Feinberg's official website, accessed January 3, 2018, http://www.lesliefeinberg.net/self/.

2. Minnie Bruce Pratt, "Transgender Pioneer and *Stone Butch Blues* Author Leslie Feinberg Has Died," *Advocate*, November 17, 2014, https://www.advocate.com/arts-entertainment/books/2014/11/17/transgender-pioneer-leslie-feinberg-stone-butch-blues-has-died.

3. Examples of scholarship in this vein are Deborah Cohler, "Afterword: Drag King Dreams Deferred," in *Citizen, Invert, Queer: Lesbianism and War in Early Twentieth-Century Britain*, by Cohler (Minneapolis: University of Minnesota Press, 2010); Jeffrey M. Dickemann, "Words, Words, Words: Talking Transgenders," *GLQ: A Journal of Lesbian and Gay Studies* 6, no. 3 (2000); Monika I. Hogan, " 'Still me on the inside, trapped': Embodied Captivity and Ethical Narrative in Leslie Feinberg's *Stone Butch Blues*," *Third Space: A Journal of Feminist Theory and Culture* 3, no. 2 (2004); Jay Prosser, "No Place Like Home: The Transgendered Narrative of Leslie Feinberg's *Stone Butch Blues*," *Modern Fiction Studies* 41, no. 3–4 (Fall-Winter 1995); Anika Stafford, "Departing Shame: Feinberg and Queer/Transgender Counter-cultural Remembering," *Journal of Gender Studies* 21, no. 3 (2012); and Jean Bobby Noble, *Masculinities without Men? Female Masculinity in Twentieth-Century Fictions* (Vancouver: UBC Press, 2004). A provocative exception is Henriette Dahan Kalev, "Sarah was a Butch: Sexual Identity, Gender Practices, and Sarah's Place as Mother in the Jewish National Pantheon," *Journal of Lesbian Studies* 16, no. 2 (2012), in which the author argues for analyzing the biblical Sarah as a butch and Feinberg in the ancient Jewish category of the *aylonit*. See also Sarra Lev, "How the *'Aylonit* Got Her Sex," *AJS Review* 31, no. 2 (2007).

4. For examples, see Albert Memmi, *The Liberation of the Jew*, trans. Judy Hyun (New York: Orion Press, 1966); Evelyn Torton Beck, "The Politics of Jewish Invisibility," *NWSA Journal* 1, no. 1 (1988); Judith Plaskow, "Blaming the Jews for the Birth of Patriarchy," in *Nice Jewish Girls: A Lesbian Anthology*, ed. Evelyn Torton Beck (Boston: Beacon Press, 1989); Abby Ferber, "The Culture of Privilege: Color-blindness, Postfeminism, and Christonormativity," *Journal of Social Issues* 68, no. 1 (2012): 64; Marla Brettschneider, *Jewish Feminism and Intersectionality* (Albany: State University of New York Press, 2016); David Hirsh, *Contemporary Left Antisemitism* (London: Routledge, 2017).

5. Leslie Feinberg, *Stone Butch Blues: A Novel* (San Francisco: Firebrand Books, 1993), 17, 19; Leslie Feinberg, *Transgender Warriors: Making History from Joan of Arc to Dennis Rodman* (Boston: Beacon Press, 1996), 49, 24–25; Leslie Feinberg, *Lavender & Red* (series), *Workers World*, 2004–2008, 40, https://www.workers.org/lavender-red/; Leslie Feinberg, *Drag King Dreams* (New York: Carroll & Graf, 2006), 260–269.

6. Feinberg's work uses the term *gay*; see Minnie Bruce Pratt, "Leslie Feinberg, a Communist Who Revolutionized Transgender Rights," *Workers World*, November 18, 2014, http://www.workers.org/articles/2014/11/18/leslie-feinberg. Feinberg had been part of leftist Jewish peace work on Israel-Palestine for many years (Feinberg, *Drag King Dreams*, 87, 103; Feinberg, *Lavender & Red*, 100). Most

US Jews are critical of Israeli government policy with regard to Palestine and the Palestinian people, despite widespread skewed understandings of their views on this matter, particularly among non-Jews. For more recent data, see Marla Brettschneider, *Cornerstones of Peace: Jewish Identity Politics and Democratic Theory* (New Brunswick, NJ: Rutgers University Press, 1996); Pew Research Center, *A Portrait of Jewish Americans: Findings from a Pew Research Center Survey of U.S. Jews*, October 1, 2013, http://www.pewforum.org/dataset/a-portrait-of-jewish-americans/.

7. Feinberg, *Transgender Warriors*, 11.

8. Feinberg, *Stone Butch Blues*, 240.

9. Feinberg, *Transgender Warriors*, 15.

10. Feinberg, *Stone Butch Blues*, 18; Feinberg, *Transgender Warriors*, 49, 50; Leslie Feinberg, *Trans Liberation: Beyond Pink or Blue* (Boston: Beacon Press, 1998), 50; Dina Pinsky, *Jewish Feminists: Complex Identities and Activist Lives* (Urbana: University of Illinois Press, 2010); Melissa R. Klapper, *Ballots, Babies, and Banners of Peace: American Jewish Women's Activism, 1890–1940* (New York: New York University Press, 2013); Joyce Antler, *Jewish Radical Feminism: Voices from the Women's Liberation Movement* (New York: New York University Press, 2018).

11. See Noble, *Masculinities*; Marla Brettschneider, "Jewish Lesbians: New Work in the Field," introduction to *Journal of Lesbian Studies* special issue, ed. Marla Brettschneider, 23, no. 1 (2019): 2–20.

12. Antler, *Jewish Radical Feminism*; Melanie Kaye/Kantrowitz, *The Issue Is Power: Essays on Women, Jews, Violence and Resistance* (San Francisco: Aunt Lute Books, 1992); Pinsky, *Jewish Feminists*; Debra L. Schultz, *Going South: Jewish Women in the Civil Rights Movement* (New York: New York University Press, 2001).

13. For example, the dialogue between the main character in *Drag King Dreams*, Max, and Hesh often references differences among Jews (91, 113, 120), particularly regarding religious/secular experiences (89–90) and Israel-Palestine politics (121, 280–81).

14. Feinberg, *Drag King Dreams*, 74, 91, 212; Pew Research Center, *Jewish Americans*.

15. Feinberg, *Lavender & Red*, 2, 5, 17–19, 35–37, 40, and *Trans Liberation*, 31; Pew Research Center, *Jewish Americans*.

16. Pew Research Center.

17. Schultz, *Going South*; Stephen Katz, *Red, Black, and Jew: New Frontiers in Hebrew Literature* (Austin: University of Texas Press, 2009).

18. Eric Goldstein, *The Price of Whiteness: Jews, Race, and American Identity* (Princeton, NJ: Princeton University Press, 2006).

19. Marla Brettschneider, *The Jewish Phenomenon in Sub-Saharan Africa: The Politics of Contradictory Discourses* (Lewiston, NY: Edwin Mellen Press, 2015).

20. Jeffrey Gorsky, *Exiles in Sepharad: The Jewish Millennium in Spain* (Philadelphia: Jewish Publication Society, 2015).

21. Feinberg references Sephardi Jewish tradition in her second novel (*Drag King Dreams*, 222).

22. Karen Brodkin, *How Jews Became White Folks and What That Says about Race in America* (New Brunswick, NJ: Rutgers University Press, 1998).

23. Kaye/Kantrowitz, *Power*.

24. Feinberg, *Stone Butch Blues*, 18, and *Rainbow Solidarity in Defense of Cuba* (New York: World View Forum, 2009), 19.

25. Feinberg, *Transgender Warriors*, 5; Marla Brettschneider, *The Family Flamboyant: Race Politics, Queer Families, Jewish Lives* (Albany: State University of New York Press, 2006).

26. Feinberg, *Transgender Warriors*, 5, 83, and *Lavender & Red*, 26, 40.

27. See the work of Jews for Racial and Economic Justice and the Jewish Multiracial Network to learn more about Jewish racialization and anti-racist work in the US.

28. This power dynamic likely also contributed to the way Feinberg notes Max's engagement with targeted Muslims (*Drag King Dreams*, 160–65).

29. Feinberg, *Lavender & Red*, 79; Pratt, "Transgender Pioneer."

30. Feinberg, *Lavender & Red*, 2, 5, 17–19, 36–37, 40, and *Trans Liberation*, 31.

31. Feinberg, *Trans Liberation*, 18, 21, 22; Theodore W. Allen, *The Invention of the White Race* (London: Verso, 1994).

32. *Drag King Dreams*, 144.

33. Brian Dolber, *Media and Culture in the U.S. Jewish Labor Movement: Sweating for Democracy in the Interwar Era* (Cham, Switzerland: Palgrave Macmillan, 2017); Bennett Muraskin, *Jews in the American Labor Movement: Past, Present and Future* (Lincolnshire, IL: International Institute for Secular Humanistic Judaism, 2016).

34. Feinberg, *Transgender Warriors*, 16, and *Lavender & Red*, 26; Gerald Horne, "Black, White, and Red: Jewish and African Americans in the Communist Party," in *The Narrow Bridge: Jewish Views on Multiculturalism*, ed. Marla Brettschneider (New Brunswick, NJ: Rutgers University Press, 1996); Dexter Jeffries, *Triple Exposure: Black, Jewish, and Red in the 1950s* (New York: Dafina Books, 2004).

35. *Lavender & Red*, 9.

36. Feinberg, *Stone Butch Blues*, 24–25, 66, and *Drag King Dreams*, 120, 144. See, for example, Kathy Ferguson's 2011 analysis of Emma Goldman's multitiered strategy of speaking in English for general anarchist, labor, and radical audiences and in Yiddish for Jewish ones, *Emma Goldman: Political Thinking in the Streets* (Lanham, MD: Rowman & Littlefield, 2011).

37. Feinberg, *Stone Butch Blues*, 66.

38. Schultz, *Going South*.

39. See Schultz, *Going South*, and continuing examples in the work of the Jewish Labor Committee and Jews for Racial and Economic Justice.

40. Feinberg, *Lavender & Red*, 57.

41. Sasha Goldberg, "Zahor: In Remembrance of Our Stone Butch Hero," *The State of the Butch Union* (blog), November 18, 2014, https://sashatgoldberg. wordpress.com/2014/11/18/zahor-in-remembrance-of-our-stone-butch-hero/.

42. Feinberg, *Stone Butch Blues*, 147–48, 173, 178, 217. See also Stafford, "Departing Shame," 303; Dickemann, "Words," 457.

43. Feinberg, *Transgender Warriors*, 67; Daniel Boyarin, *Unheroic Conduct: The Rise of Heterosexuality and the Invention of the Jewish Man* (Berkeley: University of California Press, 1997); Daniel Boyarin, Daniel Itzkovitz, and Ann Pellegrini, eds., *Queer Theory and the Jewish Question* (New York: Columbia University Press, 2003); Brettschneider, *Family*; Naomi Seidman, *A Marriage Made in Heaven: The Sexual Politics of Hebrew and Yiddish* (Berkeley: University of California Press, 1997).

44. Feinberg, *Stone Butch Blues*, 158; Cressida J. Heyes, "Feminist Solidarity after Queer Theory: The Case of Transgender Author(s)," *Signs: Journal of Women in Culture and Society* 28, no. 4 (2003).

45. Feinberg, *Trans Liberation*, 21; Heath Fogg Davis, *Beyond Trans: Does Gender Matter?* (New York: New York University Press, 2017).

46. Feinberg's protagonist in *Stone Butch Blues* struggles with this explicitly. See, for example, 139, 147–48, 173, 178, 217, and *Drag King Dreams*, 4. See also Pratt, "Transgender Pioneer."

47. See Lev, " 'Aylonit," and "They Treat Him as a Man and See Him as a Woman: The Tannaitic Understanding of the Congenital Eunuch," *Jewish Studies Quarterly* 17, no. 3 (2010); Naomi Seidman, "Reading 'Queer' Ashkenaz: This Time from East to West," *The Drama Review* 55, no. 3 (2011); Max Strassfeld, "Translating the Human," *Transgender Studies Quarterly* 3, no. 3–4 (2016), and *Trans Talmud: Androgynes and Eunichs in Rabbinic Literature* (Oakland: University of California Press, 2022); and Sarra Lev and Rona Matlow in this volume.

48. Feinberg, *Trans Liberation*, 56–58, 66.

49. Seidman, *Marriage*; Nancy Ordover, *American Eugenics: Race, Queer Anatomy, and the Science of Nationalism* (Minneapolis: University of Minnesota Press, 2003).

50. Feinberg, *Trans Liberation*, 146, and *Lavender & Red*, 57.

51. Pratt, "Transgender Pioneer."

52. Feinberg, *Lavender & Red*, 37, 39, 41.

53. Feinberg, *Stone Butch Blues*, 24–25, 67; *Transgender Warriors*, 5, 67; *Lavender & Red*, 79.

54. Feinberg, *Stone Butch Blues*, 296, and *Lavender & Red*, 38, 39.

55. Feinberg, *Lavender & Red*, 17–19; Martha Ackelsberg, "Toward a Multicultural Politics: A Jewish Feminist Perspective," in Brettschneider, *Narrow Bridge*, 89–104.

56. Stuart Svonkin, *Jews against Prejudice: American Jews and the Fight for Civil Liberties* (New York: Columbia University Press, 1997); Or N. Rose, Jo Ellen

Green Kaiser, and Margie Klein, *Righteous Indignation: A Jewish Call for Justice* (Nashville: Turner Publishing, 2008); Muraskin, *Labor Movement*.

57. See also Klapper, *Ballots* (with Feinberg, *Trans Liberation*, 52) as an example. Historically, Jewish women and feminists engaged extensively in public political activism in a range of progressive to radical movements, such as those calling for suffrage, birth control, and peace. They did this work both within the US Jewish community and with a host of organizations that were not explicitly Jewish. Similarly, Jewish women were politically active not only in Jewish women's and feminist groups but also within numerous cross-gendered Jewish organizations.

58. *Rainbow Solidarity*, 93–94; *Lavender & Red*, 100.

59. In *Rainbow Solidarity* this is less so.

References

Ackelsberg, Martha. "Toward a Multicultural Politics: A Jewish Feminist Perspective." In *The Narrow Bridge: Jewish Views on Multiculturalism*, edited by Marla Brettschneider, 89–104. New Brunswick, NJ: Rutgers University Press, 1996.

Allen, Theodore W. *The Invention of the White Race*. London: Verso, 1994.

Antler, Joyce. *Jewish Radical Feminism: Voices from the Women's Liberation Movement*. New York: New York University Press, 2018.

Beck, Evelyn Torton. *Nice Jewish Girls: A Lesbian Anthology*. Berkeley, CA: The Crossing Press, 1982.

———. "The Politics of Jewish Invisibility." *NWSA Journal* 1, no. 1 (1988): 93–102.

Boyarin, Daniel. *Unheroic Conduct: The Rise of Heterosexuality and the Invention of the Jewish Man*. Berkeley: University of California Press, 1997.

Boyarin, Daniel, Daniel Itzkovitz, and Ann Pellegrini, eds. *Queer Theory and the Jewish Question*. New York: Columbia University Press, 2003.

Brettschneider, Marla. *Cornerstones of Peace: Jewish Identity Politics and Democratic Theory*. New Brunswick, NJ: Rutgers University Press, 1996.

———. *The Family Flamboyant: Race Politics, Queer Families, Jewish Lives*. Albany: State University of New York Press, 2006.

———. *Jewish Feminism and Intersectionality*. Albany: State University of New York Press, 2016.

———. "Jewish Lesbians: New Work in the Field." Introduction to *Journal of Lesbian Studies* special issue, edited by Marla Brettschneider, 23, no. 1 (2019): 2–20.

———. *The Jewish Phenomenon in Sub-Saharan Africa: The Politics of Contradictory Discourses*. Lewiston, NY: Edwin Mellen Press, 2015.

Brodkin, Karen. *How Jews Became White Folks and What That Says about Race in America*. New Brunswick, NJ: Rutgers University Press, 1998.

Bulkin, Elly, Minnie Bruce Pratt, and Barbara Smith. *Yours in Struggle: Three Feminist Perspectives of Anti-semitism and Racism*. New York: Long Haul Press, 1984.

Cohler, Deborah. "Afterword: Drag King Dreams Deferred." In *Citizen, Invert, Queer: Lesbianism and War in Early Twentieth-Century Britain*, by Deborah Cohler, 197–209. Minneapolis: University of Minnesota Press, 2010.

Davis, Heath Fogg. *Beyond Trans: Does Gender Matter?* New York: New York University Press, 2017.

Dickemann, Jeffrey M. "Words, Words, Words: Talking Transgenders." *GLQ: A Journal of Lesbian and Gay Studies* 6, no. 3 (2000): 455–66.

Dolber, Brian. *Media and Culture in the U.S. Jewish Labor Movement: Sweating for Democracy in the Interwar Era*. Cham, Switzerland: Palgrave Macmillan, 2017.

Feinberg, Leslie. *Drag King Dreams*. New York: Carroll & Graf, 2006.

———. *Lavender & Red* (series). *Workers World*, 2004–2008. https://www.workers.org/lavender-red/.

———. *Rainbow Solidarity in Defense of Cuba*. New York: World View Forum, 2009.

———. *Stone Butch Blues: A Novel*. San Francisco: Firebrand Books, 1993.

———. *Transgender Warriors: Making History from Joan of Arc to Dennis Rodman*. Boston: Beacon Press, 1996.

———. *Trans Liberation: Beyond Pink or Blue*. Boston: Beacon Press, 1998.

Ferber, Abby. "The Culture of Privilege: Color-blindness, Postfeminism, and Christonormativity." *Journal of Social Issues* 68, no. 1 (2012): 63–77.

Ferguson, Kathy. *Emma Goldman: Political Thinking in the Streets*. Lanham, MD: Rowman & Littlefield, 2011.

Goldberg, Sasha. "Zahor: In Remembrance of Our Stone Butch Hero." *The State of the Butch Union* (blog), November 18, 2014. https://sashatgoldberg.wordpress.com/2014/11/18/zahor-in-remembrance-of-our-stone-butch-hero/.

Goldstein, Eric. *The Price of Whiteness: Jews, Race, and American Identity*. Princeton, NJ: Princeton University Press, 2006.

Gorsky, Jeffrey. *Exiles in Sepharad: The Jewish Millennium in Spain*. Philadelphia: Jewish Publication Society, 2015.

Heyes, Cressida J. "Feminist Solidarity after Queer Theory: The Case of Transgender Author(s)." *Signs: Journal of Women in Culture and Society* 28, no. 4 (2003): 1093–120.

Hirsh, David. *Contemporary Left Antisemitism*. London: Routledge, 2017.

Hogan, Monika I. " 'Still me on the inside, trapped': Embodied Captivity and Ethical Narrative in Leslie Feinberg's *Stone Butch Blues*." *Third Space: A Journal of Feminist Theory and Culture* 3, no. 2 (2004).

Horne, Gerald. "Black, White, and Red: Jewish and African Americans in the Communist Party." In *The Narrow Bridge: Jewish Views on Multiculturalism*, edited by Marla Brettschneider, 123–35. New Brunswick, NJ: Rutgers University Press, 1996.

Jeffries, Dexter. *Triple Exposure: Black, Jewish, and Red in the 1950s*. New York: Dafina Books, 2004.

Kalev, Henriette Dahan. "Sarah was a Butch: Sexual Identity, Gender Practices, and Sarah's Place as Mother in the Jewish National Pantheon." *Journal of Lesbian Studies* 16, no. 2 (2012): 220–37.

Katz, Stephen. *Red, Black, and Jew: New Frontiers in Hebrew Literature*. Austin: University of Texas Press, 2009.

Kaye/Kantrowitz, Melanie. *The Issue Is Power: Essays on Women, Jews, Violence and Resistance*. San Francisco: Aunt Lute Books, 1992.

Kaye/Kantrowitz, Melanie, and Irena Klepfisz. *The Tribe of Dina: A Jewish Women's Anthology*. Boston: Beacon Press, 1986.

Klapper, Melissa R. *Ballots, Babies, and Banners of Peace: American Jewish Women's Activism, 1890–1940*. New York: New York University Press, 2013.

Lev, Sarra. "How the 'Aylonit Got Her Sex." *AJS Review* 31, no. 2 (2007): 297–316.

———. "They Treat Him as a Man and See Him as a Woman: The Tannaitic Understanding of the Congenital Eunuch." *Jewish Studies Quarterly* 17, no. 3 (2010): 213–43.

Litman, Jane, and Jakob Hero-Shaw. *Liberating Gender for Jews and Allies: The Wisdom of Transkeit*. Newcastle upon Tyne, UK: Cambridge Scholars Publishing, 2022.

Memmi, Albert. *The Liberation of the Jew*. Translated by Judy Hyun. New York: Orion Press, 1966.

Muraskin, Bennett. *Jews in the American Labor Movement: Past, Present and Future*. Lincolnshire, IL: International Institute for Secular Humanistic Judaism, 2016.

Noble, Jean Bobby. *Masculinities without Men? Female Masculinity in Twentieth-Century Fictions*. Vancouver: UBC Press, 2004.

Ordover, Nancy. *American Eugenics: Race, Queer Anatomy, and the Science of Nationalism*. Minneapolis: University of Minnesota Press, 2003.

Pew Research Center. *A Portrait of Jewish Americans: Findings from a Pew Research Center Survey of U.S. Jews*. October 1, 2013. http://www.pewforum.org/dataset/a-portrait-of-jewish-americans/.

Pinsky, Dina. *Jewish Feminists: Complex Identities and Activist Lives*. Urbana: University of Illinois Press, 2010.

Plaskow, Judith. "Blaming the Jews for the Birth of Patriarchy." In *Nice Jewish Girls: A Lesbian Anthology*, edited by Evelyn Torton Beck, 298–302. Boston: Beacon Press, 1989.

Pratt, Minnie Bruce. "Transgender Pioneer and *Stone Butch Blues* Author Leslie Feinberg Has Died." *Advocate*, November 17, 2014. https://www.advocate.com/arts-entertainment/books/2014/11/17/transgender-pioneer-leslie-feinberg-stone-butch-blues-has-died.

Prosser, Jay. "No Place Like Home: The Transgendered Narrative of Leslie Feinberg's *Stone Butch Blues*." *Modern Fiction Studies* 41, no. 3–4 (Fall-Winter 1995): 483–514.

Rose, Or N., Jo Ellen Green Kaiser, and Margie Klein. *Righteous Indignation: A Jewish Call for Justice*. Nashville: Turner Publishing, 2008.

Schultz, Debra L. *Going South: Jewish Women in the Civil Rights Movement*. New York: New York University Press, 2001.

Seidman, Naomi. *A Marriage Made in Heaven: The Sexual Politics of Hebrew and Yiddish*. Berkeley: University of California Press, 1997.

———. "Reading 'Queer' Ashkenaz: This Time from East to West." *The Drama Review* 55, no. 3 (2011): 50–56.

Stafford, Anika. "Departing Shame: Feinberg and Queer/Transgender Counter-cultural Remembering." *Journal of Gender Studies* 21, no. 3 (2012): 301–12.

Strassfeld, Max. "Translating the Human." *Transgender Studies Quarterly* 3, no. 3–4 (2016): 587–604.

———. *Trans Talmud: Androgynes and Eunichs in Rabbinic Literature*. Oakland: University of California Press, 2022.

Svonkin, Stuart. *Jews against Prejudice: American Jews and the Fight for Civil Liberties*. New York: Columbia University Press, 1997.

Chapter 12

Postmodern Concepts of Sex, Gender, and Sexuality in the Framework of the Jewish Lesbian

Rona B. Matlow

Introduction

In a recent tragic event familiar to most in the United States, a so-called "gender reveal" stunt went horribly wrong.[1] This stunt utilized an incendiary device to indicate the assigned sex in utero of the baby the mother was carrying. Sadly, this device sparked the El Dorado wildland fire, which led to the death of a firefighter. Because of this, the parents will likely face charges of manslaughter, with the possibility of the baby being born in prison and going into the child welfare system.

Such stunts are a farce, because these so-called gender reveals actually reveal assigned sex, not gender (as we will explore later), because the child cannot know its gender until it is sentient. This is not the first time such a stunt has led to a death.[2] Such stunts show the enormous lack of understanding of sex and gender as well as the lack of personal responsibility that are, sadly, emblematic of the year 2020.

In this chapter, I will explore sex and gender identity to help the reader understand sexuality more clearly, because without a clear understanding of the former it is impossible to understand the latter.

The Tanakh Shows Nonbinary Identity!

I've stated that the binary does not technically exist. This is a Jewish anthology. I will first explore some Jewish texts to show the tradition of nonbinary identity in classical texts. I will begin with Genesis 1:27:[3]

כז וַיִּבְרָ֨א אֱלֹקִ֤ים ׀ אֶת־הָֽאָדָם֙ בְּצַלְמ֔וֹ
בְּצֶ֥לֶם אֱלֹקִ֖ים בָּרָ֣א אֹת֑וֹ
זָכָ֥ר וּנְקֵבָ֖ה בָּרָ֥א אֹתָֽם׃

God created The Adam in the Divine image
In the Divine image God created The Adam
Male *and* female, God created them.[4]

I have deliberately parsed this text in three parts. The first two show a chiastic parallel: *a* then *b*; *b* then *a*. The essential point is that this doubles the assertion that The Adam (humanity) is created in the Divine image.[5] We know that God is incorporeal (having no body). But if, for argument's sake, we were to presume that God *might* have a body, then any characteristic of God would have infinite possibility. We are talking assigned sex here, so God would have infinite possibility of assigned sex. Thus, if God has infinite possibility of assigned sex and The Adam is created in God's image (a point that is doubled for emphasis), then The Adam *must* also have infinite possibility of assigned sex!

In the third part of the verse, we see that The Adam is created *both* male and female. This is confirmed by the two curved lines (cantillation marks) under the Hebrew text. This indicates a merism, all possible assigned sexes, not just male and female. Since The Adam is a metaphor for humanity, this makes sense. Bereshit Rabbah 8:1 on this verse states that The Adam was a single entity with two faces (male and female), similar to the Platonic soulmate.[6]

Another important point to note about "male and female, God created <u>them</u>" is that this does not mean that God created men and women at this point in the creative story. This verse is discussing The Adam, a metaphor for humanity. The Adam, as I have shown, is a single, androgynous entity. "Them" at the end of this verse refers to the infinite possible sexes (genders) of The Adam, the human being. It does not mean that God created Adam and Eve, yet that is the common reading by people who are unable to access the traditional Jewish sources.

The study of the creation of humanity is not complete without exploring the separation of The Adam into Adam and Eve. This is found in Genesis 2:21:

וַיַּפֵּל יְהֹוָה אֱלֹהִים ׀ תַּרְדֵּמָה עַל־הָאָדָם וַיִּישָׁן וַיִּקַּח אַחַת מִצַּלְעֹתָיו וַיִּסְגֹּר בָּשָׂר תַּחְתֶּנָּה:

H' God caused a great sleep to fall on The Adam and he slept, and (God) took one of (The Adam's) sides, and (God) closed the flesh under her.

I have translated this as "side," not rib, which is the common Christian translation. I base this on Rashi's exegesis of this verse:

מִצַּלְעֹתָיו. מִסְּטָרָיו, כְּמוֹ וּלְצֶלַע הַמִּשְׁכָּן

From their side, like "and to the side of the Mishkan" [portable Tabernacle].

I have rendered בשר תחתנה as "the flesh under her" because the declination of the last word is in the feminine. Clearly both Adam and Eve would have needed their surgical sites closed, however. The Hebrew word צלע can mean "rib" or "side," but in Jewish textual interpretation it means "side." This is of vital importance because, unlike in Christian theology, where women bear the taint of Original Sin, in Jewish theology, women and men are created equally.

In the Hebrew Bible, nonbinary language is not overt, but nonbinary sex and gender can be read into the text in many places, and many scholars have done so.[7] It is, at times, dependent on translation techniques.[8]

The Early Rabbis Teach Diversity

When we then move forward to the midrash on this text, Bereshit Rabbah 8:1, it states, "when God created the First Adam, God created them Androgynous, as it is written male *and* female God created them." Please note that in rabbinic parlance *androgynous* refers to a person who is assigned with indeterminate genitalia (or both penis and vulva) at birth. I will come back to this later.

The next text to consider is from Mishnah Sanhedrin 4:5: "When a coin maker stamps a coin with his die, all the coins are identical. To tell the greatness of the Holy Blessing One, when God stamps humanity from God's single die, every human is unique." From this Mishnah, with every human being unique, we must then presume that every characteristic that each person has is unique, and different from every other person.

Thus, we see from multiple paths that humanity was created with infinite possibility of sex: from God's image, from the literary analysis, from the Masoretic text and merism, and from the midrashim found in Genesis Rabbah and Mishnah Sanhedrin.

I will now explore how the rabbis of the Talmud saw assigned sex.[9] They offered six possible assigned sexes for theoretical consideration. This is not to say that these sexes actually existed but that they used these as tools for halakhic (Jewish law) exploration. Most, if not all, are known today, but the rabbis likely did not actually know of them. Nonetheless, that the rabbis considered six assigned sexes was extremely radical for two thousand years ago.

Also, keep in mind that assigned sex simply means a visual, external look at genitalia of a baby upon birth. There is no internal exam; there are no DNA tests. When anti-trans activists talk about biological sex, they are incorrect, because assigned sex can be completely unrelated to DNA.

The six sexes the rabbis explore throughout the Talmud are[10]

zakhar—assigned male at birth
nekeivah—assigned female at birth
androgynous—assigned with ambiguous genitalia (or both penis and vulva) at birth
tumtum—assigned with no visible genitalia at birth
saris—assigned male at birth but lost the ability to procreate (note that there are two subcategories: hama, or natural, and adam, or caused by human action)
aylonit—assigned female at birth but lost the ability to procreate

I should note that the rabbis' use of tumtum and androgynous was primarily for theoretical constructs. They were likely not aware of any actual cases of these identities. Rather, they used them to develop questions of halakhah, of Jewish Law. Commonly, the belief is that the tumtum is totally theoretical; however, there have been some cases recorded of people who met the criteria to be designated a tumtum.[11] The Talmudic tractate Yevamot explores the cases of the *tumtum*, *androgynous*, and *saris* very deeply.[12]

The bottom line of this section is that rabbis of the Mishnah, midrash, and Talmud saw that assigned sex is *anything but* binary. In antiquity, and in fact up until the modern era, sex and gender were not actually separate concepts. Gender roles were determined by a person's sex, and that was all people really knew. Gender, the internal sense of one's identity, which may or may not align with one's assigned sex, therefore cannot in any way be binary. From this perspective, the notion of a sex-gender binary is preposterous.

Sexuality Is Not Clear-Cut or Binary Either

As this chapter addresses Jewish sexuality, we must of course explore the most challenging text in Judaism regarding sexuality, Leviticus 18:22:

וְאֶת-זָכָר לֹא תִשְׁכַּב מִשְׁכְּבֵי אִשָּׁה תּוֹעֵבָה הִוא:

> And you, [cisgender] male, shall not have [penetrating] sex with another [cisgender] male in all the ways of having [penetrating] sex with a [cisgender] female; it is an abomination.

This original translation of mine represents a deliberate process to convey all the nuances of the Hebrew, including sex identity, for those not familiar with biblical Hebrew scholarship. This is, of course, dramatically different than the familiar "you shall not lie with a man as with a woman . . . ."

I would note that cisgender men have two paths for penetrating sex (oral and anal) and cisgender women have three (oral, vaginal, and anal). Given this, how exactly can cisgender men have penetrating sex in *all the ways* of cisgender women? This is an ambiguity that orthodox religionists of all Abrahamic religions gloss over.

But classical Torah commentator Abraham Ibn Ezra, who lived in Spain and Arab lands during the twelfth century, offers a radical possibility:

כי יש מי שיחדש בגופו כצורת בשר אשה וזה לא יתכן בתולדה. וי»א אנדרוגינוס.

> For there could be a person who changes the form of his flesh to the form of a woman, but this could never happen naturally. And some say it is an androgynous person.

This is radical. Ibn Ezra is offering the possible understanding that a man could undergo gender confirmation surgery at some point in his life. He rules this out as a possibility because it isn't possible in nature. Note he says תולדה, *toldah*, which is typically understood as "generations" but in this instance is read as "nature." But it could be read as "in our (i.e., his) time" (that is, the twelfth century). However, this process is certainly possible in modern times. I had it done in 2018!

A strictly literal reading of this verse shows that penetrating sex between men in all the ways of sex with a woman is seemingly impossible. Further, this classical commentary suggests a viable alternative to a prohibition on gay sex. There is yet another alternative understanding.

The classical rules of biblical exegesis come from the Baraita of Rabbi Yishmael (an introduction to the halakhic midrash Sifra). Rule 12 states that an inference may be made from the context of the verse or the adjacent verse. The preceding verse, Leviticus 18:21, prohibits child sacrifice. The following verse, Leviticus 18:23, prohibits bestiality. By this rule, we might then infer that our verse is a prohibition of a specific pagan cultic ritual. We already know from Leviticus 18:5ff. that Jews are prohibited from following pagan ritual practices.

Thus, from this brief excursus, there are three possible alternative understandings of Leviticus 18:22. None of us were present when the Torah was written, so we cannot know the original intent of the text. However, we can, with some certainty, infer that it is not a prohibition on committed sex between two male partners.

In antiquity, when sexuality was not a known construct, the concern was people staying within the constraints of their sex (gender) roles. Thus, although in Greco-Roman society the *kinaidos* was tolerated, there were those who looked down upon him.[13]

This present chapter pertains to lesbians, however. The Hebrew Bible does not directly address women's sexuality, except to show many times over that it is controlled by their fathers or husbands. But what of lesbians? We must go to rabbinic writings for that.

In the Talmud, tractate Yevamot 76a, we find the following discussion regarding women who engage in sexual play and whether they are fit to marry a man from the priestly class afterward (i.e., are they still considered a virgin?).

> Thus says Rabbi Huna: women who rub against each other vaginally are prohibited from marrying into the priestly class [because such conduct renders them a *zona* (whore)]. But even

Rabbi Elazar disagrees; as he says, a man who has intercourse with a woman for the sake of other than marriage renders the woman a *zona*; this is **only** with a man. If she has sex with another woman, it is only licentiousness and does not render her a *zona*. [Thus she is still fit to marry a man in the priestly class.]

Maimonides, in his code, the *Mishneh Torah*, writes thus (Laws of Sex 21:8):

Women rubbing against each other sexually is prohibited, and this is an act of Egypt that is warned against in Torah, saying, "Do not do the acts of Egypt." The sages asked, "What did they do? A man married a man, and a woman married a woman, a woman married two men." Even though this [lesbian] act is prohibited, we do not give them lashes because there is no specific [Torah] prohibition, and it isn't truly an act of sexual intercourse. Therefore, she is not prohibited from marrying into the priestly class because of harlotry.

The later codes mirror this. From this we may infer that while the rabbis do not approve of lesbian sex, there is no prohibition against it. It may, in general, violate rules of modesty and other conduct codes applicable to the times of the Talmud and codes, but we live in different times, and social mores have changed.

In modern times, orthodoxy still prohibits lesbian sex, but there are plenty of lesbians and other queer people in the orthodox world. The organization Eshel (www.eshel.org) is a social organization for LGBTQ Orthodox Jews.

Modern Issues of Lesbian Sexuality

Now that we have taken a survey of Jewish texts on sex, gender, and sexuality, it is time to explore the issues of the language of lesbian sexuality. The categories typically assigned to LGBTQ (or queer, if you prefer) people, such as *gay*, *lesbian*, *bisexual*, *transgender*, and so on, were assigned to us largely by the cisgender-heterosexual binary (i.e., the straight world) to put us in boxes.

Feminist scholars such as Judith Butler and Monique Wittig have explored the limitations that legacy language places on identity and what nonbinary language of **sexuality** might mean. "The fact that identities are always based on sets of exclusions has hitherto determined the binary ways in which they are thought (i.e., I am this because I am not that)."[14] However, they have not truly explored nonbinary **gender** with sexuality in the way that I am exploring it.

In feminist studies, we work to break boxes and break the glass ceiling. In Black studies, people work to break the bonds of racism. In the queer world, we work to break those *and* all the bonds of queer-phobia, whatever they may be, as well as ableism. A large part of that includes reframing language. Michael Bronski frames an excellent history of the development of the language used to describe LGBTQ people, from Church language through the medieval period to early and modern queer usage.[15] During the days prior to understanding nonbinary identity, this was easy: homosexual women were lesbians. Or was it?

Let's take my story as an example. For the first fifty-five years of my life, I pretended to be male. It wasn't until 2015 that I finally figured out that I was a woman and transitioned. However, my sexuality did not change—I was attracted to women prior to and after transition. By the classical definition, that makes me a lesbian (a woman attracted to another woman).

I identify as a genderpunk nonbinary disabled elder transgender woman veteran rabbi. *Genderpunk* is synonymous with *genderfuck*; its usage goes back to the 1960s and 1970s.[16] Tommi Avicolli Mecca writes, "Many of the gay liberationists I met were into radical drag (also known as genderfuck), a form of political dress that mocked traditional roles. Its purposes were to show people how arbitrary gender-specific dress and behavior were and to free up men and women to be themselves."[17] The first appearance of the term *genderfuck* is attributed to Christopher Lonc; he is reported to have said, "I want to criticize and poke fun at the roles of women and of men too. I want to try and show how not-normal I can be. I want to ridicule and destroy the whole cosmology of restrictive sex roles and sexual identification."[18]

I use ze/hir pronouns.[19] Why? When I wear a button that says "ze/hir," people ask about it, and that opens an opportunity for dialogue. I adhere to these identities because I do not believe that a sex or gender binary exists.

Once we have reframed the language of how we identify our genders, then we *must* reframe the language of sexual attraction as well. *Straight* and *gay* may have worked for binary gender identities, but they completely fall apart for nonbinary identities. Alternative language such as *androsexual* and *gynosexual* indicates attraction to men or women irrespective of one's own gender identity, as explained in the research.[20] But that only works if the person you are attracted to is binary. What if you are attracted to someone who is nonbinary?

Bisexual originally meant attracted to both sexes (genders)—men and women. In modern usage, it now means attracted to more than one gender to account for the vagaries of nonbinary identity, but even this has been found lacking, as Corey Flanders explores.[21] Some in the nonbinary world now use *bi/pansexual*. *Pansexual* refers to one who is attracted to people of all or many possible gender identities. *Bi/pan* attempts to reframe it to put some limitation on the universal nature of pansexuality, that is, less than all possibilities. Amney Harper and Renae Swanson have proposed another alternative, *polysexual*, or attracted to many genders.[22]

In my case, I could be framed as bi/pansexual or as trixic.[23] I'm attracted to women and various nonbinary people, but not men. But, if the gender binary doesn't exist, what does it mean to say I'm not attracted to "men"? What is man, since *man* is a binary term? How do you put a limit on it? It's all very fuzzy. In the end, what it comes down to is that we know who we like and who we don't, and that's fine.

Those of us in the group commonly identified as lesbian are not normatively attracted to those in the group commonly identified as male. But what if you're a classical bisexual but primarily lesbian? See how complicated this gets?

I am acquainted with several elder lesbians who now identify as nonbinary but previously struggled with their identities because they had no language to describe who they were. Even five years ago they did not. They had to be creative in how to adapt the title *lesbian* to fit their identities, because one size does not fit all.

But it gets more complicated than that. In the twenty-first century, a number of lesbians have transitioned to transgender men. While there are no clear statistics on this because transgender men are not widely studied, in 2000, the Michigan Womyn's Music Festival banned people assigned female at birth who presented as male.[24]

A famous case is that of Jacob Anderson-Minshall. His wife is Diane Anderson-Minshall, managing editor of Pride Media, including *Out* and *Advocate* magazines.[25] They married as Diane and Suzy, but Jacob transitioned. They stayed married. Now they *appear* as a heterosexual couple.[26] They worked through issues and report they are more in love than ever.

As we have already seen, there is newer language for attraction to women, such as *gynosexual* and *gynophilic*.[27] These terms work if one is a nonbinary femme or a transgender woman and attracted to a binary woman. But what if the person one is attracted to is nonbinary? Or what if one is attracted to a range of gender identities? We have already seen that no single gender identity occupies more than a point, so one would need to define a space to occupy.

One might say that they are androphobic, but this also has drawbacks. First, this is a negative term, and people prefer to deal in positive terms. Second, it is very vague. With nonbinary people, such as butch lesbians, where in the distribution of space do they lie? They could conceivably occupy a point in the half of space that would be considered "male" under the binary system.

And where is the distinction between a very butch lesbian and a transgender man? Is it only if the person declares that they are transgender? What if others perceive them as such? But these are applications of binary terms to a nonbinary reality.

In the end, each individual woman or femme-identified person will have to create or utilize extant language that feels right for them at that point in time to describe their sexuality. They must also recognize that this language is a moving target. In the short time I have been studying this language, it has changed tremendously, and it will continue to do so.

Beth Greenfield's article recounts the very latest as of this writing in what Gen Z queer people are saying as to language for gender identity and sexuality. But this is not the last or the be all and end all. The language will continue to evolve as new generations of young queer adults take the stage.

Conclusions

There is no binary in sex or gender and never actually has been. The binary is a false construct that has been misconstrued and applied by society over the millennia. Due to the application of a binary in gender, a language of sexuality developed that was simultaneously simple and complex to use and at the same time inaccurate.

Along with the recognition that gender is not binary, new language continues to develop. This adds complexity and nuance to the understanding of the sociology and psychology of gender and sexuality. At the same time, it gives individuals much more freedom to self-define.

Classical Jewish texts did not clearly define a sex and gender binary even though a binary system of gender roles was in place. The Hebrew Bible tells of men and women and does in some cases place restrictions on women or assign roles to men that women cannot fulfill, but it does not explicitly define gender or sex. The rabbinic texts define six sexes, as shown above, in order to determine the law in various cases. The Church relied primarily on the Latin rendering of the Vulgate by St. Jerome to determine what was said in the Hebrew Bible. Because, as Naomi Seidman explains, it is impossible to clearly translate an ancient language to another language, many inaccuracies were inserted. Further, Jerome was relying on the written text only, whereas Judaism relies on the written Torah as well as the oral tradition that came along with it, which is found in the Mishnah, midrash, Talmud, and various commentaries. Because of this, Church priests did not have the knowledge the rabbis did to interpret the Hebrew Bible correctly. This allowed changes such as "rib" instead of "side," described above, to be inserted. This also allowed Gen. 1:27 to be understood as the creation of Adam and Eve rather than The Adam. To sum it up, nuance is lost in the translation.

At the time of the revelation of the Hebrew Bible, a form of male homosexual sex may have been prohibited, but we do not know what it was. In our present time, it seems apparent that permissive sex between two men should be allowed by Jewish law. Further, in the commentary on this biblical text, gender confirmation surgery was envisioned in the twelfth century. There is no explicit biblical or rabbinic prohibition against two women having sex together, despite rabbinic objections to the practice.

We will continue to gain new insights into gender and sexuality as new scholars grow and learn in the field.[28]

Notes

1. Marisa Peñaloza, "A Firefighter Is Killed in California Wildfire Sparked by Gender Reveal Party," *NPR*, September 18, 2020, https://www.npr.org/2020/09/18/914368098/a-firefighter-is-killed-in-california-wildfire-sparked-by-gender-reveal-party.

2. Sandra Garcia, "Explosion at Gender Reveal Party Kills Woman, Officials Say," *New York Times*, October 28, 2019, https://www.nytimes.com/2019/10/28/us/gender-reveal-party-death.html.

3. A number of authors and scholars have explored this topic. I am not aware of many scholars who go deeply into the commentaries and analysis of the classical texts, save for Daniel Boyarin, *Carnal Israel: Reading Sex in Talmudic*

Culture (Berkeley: University of California Press, 1995), but even Boyarin does not take it as far as I do, as proving nonbinary identity is not his thesis. Further, because I am addressing the topic of the language of sexuality building on top of developing a deep understanding of nonbinary identity, this creates a totally new study.

4. Emphasis mine. Note that the Hebrew האדם The Adam," refers to a single entity, not two people. Also note that all translations are mine unless otherwise stated.

5. Note that I write "The Adam" because the Hebrew is האדם, which is a name, and this is a distinct being, different from אדם, Adam, the person whose wife was Eve. The Adam is also known as אדם הראשון, The Original Adam, in rabbinic texts.

6. On Plato's soulmate, see Aristophanes's *Symposium*.

7. One classical example of nonbinary language in the Bible is found in Numbers 5:3, in a discussion of sending contaminated males and females outside the camp. The Hebrew is מזכר עד נקבה, which most translate as "males and females." This is a sense-for-sense translation. The word-for-word translation would be "from male until female." Knowing this, the commentator of *HaKtav VeHaKabalah* (a nineteenth-century opponent of Reform Judaism) reads this as כי הזכר והנקבה הם הקצות והוא מה שביניהם, "the male and the female are the endpoints, and he is what is in the middle of them," referring to the *androgynous* or the *tumtum*. In other words, he sees in this a spectrum of possible sex present in the Israelite camp.

8. For a discussion of word-for-word and sense-for-sense translations, see Naomi Seidman, *Faithful Renderings: Jewish–Christian Difference and the Politics of Translation* (Chicago: University of Chicago Press, 2006), 73–75.

9. Please note that this is rabbinic rather than scriptural work. In scripture, two sexes are primarily presented, yet many scholars have shown evidence of nonbinary gender in scripture by reading certain language traits as well as character traits throughout the Hebrew Bible.

10. Elliot Kukla, "Terms for Gender Diversity in Classical Jewish Texts," *TransTorah*, 2006, http://www.transtorah.org/PDFs/Classical_Jewish_Terms_for_Gender_Diversity.pdf.

11. See Leah DeVun, *The Shape of Sex: Nonbinary Gender from Genesis to the Renaissance* (New York: Columbia University Press, 2021), 120, for such a case. While DeVun does not directly relate this case to the *tumtum*, I have discussed it with her, and she stated that in retrospect she wishes she had.

12. For a current study of these identities, see Max K. Strassfeld, *Trans Talmud: Androgynes and Eunuchs in Rabbinic Literature* (Oakland: University of California Press, 2022).

13. A man who acted in a sexually submissive way and was penetrated by a dominant male was called a *kinaidos*. See Brooke Holmes, *Gender: Antiquity and Its Legacy* (New York: I. B. Taurus, 2012), 93, for a thorough discussion of

this topic. The prohibition found in Lev. 18:22 is classically seen by the rabbis as a prohibition against a male being penetrated and thus changing their role to a more female-like posture. They likely knew of the *kinaidos* identity, and it no doubt influenced their feelings on making the halakhah in this case. Further, in the discussions of sex with an *androgynous* in the Talmud, the rabbis rule that they must act as a male. If an *androgynous* is penetrated rather than doing the penetrating during sex, the rabbis rule it a violation of Lev. 18:22. See Strassfeld, *Trans Talmud*, for a thorough investigation of this topic.

14. Levi C. R. Hord, "Specificity without Identity: Articulating Post-Gender Sexuality through the 'Non-binary Lesbian,'" *Sexualities* 25, no. 5–6 (2022), https://doi.org/10.1177/1363460720981564, published ahead of print, December 25, 2020, p. 9.

15. Michael Bronski, *A Queer History of the United States* (Boston: Beacon Press, 2011), xiv–xx. When using *Church* with a capital *C*, I am referring to the Roman Catholic Church specifically.

16. Mica, "What Is Genderpunk?," Ace Alliance community, Amino, accessed July 26, 2022, https://aminoapps.com/c/acealliance/page/item/genderpunk/bN2a_zR7snIXG6GnqrjdkljxPrPm25pjRvn.

17. Tommi Avicolli Mecca, "Brushes with Lily Law," in *The Stonewall Reader*, ed. New York Public Library (New York: Penguin Books, 2019), 253.

18. Quoted in David Bergman, *Camp Grounds: Style and Homosexuality* (Amherst: University of Massachusetts Press, 1993), 7.

19. Shige Sakurai, "'Ze' Pronouns," MyPronouns.org, January 22, 2017, https://www.mypronouns.org/ze-hir.

20. Claire Gillespie, "What Is Gynesexual? How Does It Differ from Gynephilia?" *Health*, October 20, 2022, https://www.health.com/mind-body/health-diversity-inclusion/gynesexual; Mattias K. Auer et al., "Transgender Transitioning and Change of Self-Reported Sexual Orientation," *PloS One* 9, no. 10 (2014): e110016, https://doi.org/10.1371/journal.pone.0110016.

21. Corey Flanders, ed., *Under the Bisexual Umbrella: Diversity of Identity and Experience* (New York: Routledge, 2019).

22. Amney J. Harper and Renae Swanson, "Nonsequential Task Model of Bi/Pan/Polysexual Identity Development," *Journal of Bisexuality* 19, no. 3 (2019): 337–60, https://doi.org/10.1080/15299716.2019.1608614.

23. Beth Greenfield, "Queer Youth Are Embracing a Flood of Labels, from 'Aceflux' to 'Xenogender.' Here's Why," *Yahoo! Life*, February 14, 2022, http://www.yahoo.com/lifestyle/queer-youth-embracing-labels-225825802.html.

24. Emi Koyama, "Frequently Asked Questions on Michigan/Trans Controversy: Introduction," *Eminism.org* (blog), http://eminism.org/michigan/faq-intro.html.

25. Diane Anderson-Minshall and Jacob Anderson-Minshall, *Queerly Beloved: A Love Story across Genders* (Valley Falls, NY: Bold Strokes Books, 2014).

26. My wife, Susan, and I have stayed married since my transition. However, opposite to the case cited, we now *appear* as a lesbian couple. In actuality, due to various issues, at this point we are both essentially asexual.

27. For an explanation of these terms, see WebMD Editorial Contributors and Dan Brennan, "What Is Gynosexuality?," WebMD (website), June 29, 2021, https://www.webmd.com/sex/what-is-gynosexuality.

28. I am grateful to Starr Hoffman, PhD, director of planning and assessment at the University of Nevada Las Vegas Libraries, and James Lawrence, PhD, DMin, director of the doctor of ministry program at the Pacific School of Religion, Berkeley, California, for their reviews of this article.

References

Anderson-Minshall, Diane, and Jacob Anderson-Minshall. *Queerly Beloved: A Love Story across Genders*. Valley Falls, NY: Bold Strokes Books, 2014.

Auer, Mattias K., Johannes Fuss, Nina Höhne, Günter K. Stalla, and Caroline Sievers. "Transgender Transitioning and Change of Self-Reported Sexual Orientation." *PloS One* 9, no. 10 (2014): e110016. https://doi.org/10.1371/journal.pone.0110016.

Bergman, David. *Camp Grounds: Style and Homosexuality*. Amherst: University of Massachusetts Press, 1993.

Boyarin, Daniel. *Carnal Israel: Reading Sex in Talmudic Culture*. Berkeley: University of California Press, 1995.

Bronski, Michael. *A Queer History of the United States*. Boston: Beacon Press, 2011.

DeVun, Leah. *The Shape of Sex: Nonbinary Gender from Genesis to the Renaissance*. New York: Columbia University Press, 2021.

Flanders, Corey, editor. *Under the Bisexual Umbrella: Diversity of Identity and Experience*. New York: Routledge, 2019.

Gillespie, Claire. "What Is Gynesexual? How Does It Differ from Gynephilia?" *Health*, October 20, 2022. https://www.health.com/mind-body/health-diversity-inclusion/gynesexual.

Harper, Amney J., and Renae Swanson. "Nonsequential Task Model of Bi/Pan/Polysexual Identity Development." *Journal of Bisexuality* 19, no. 3 (2019): 337–60. https://doi.org/10.1080/15299716.2019.1608614.

Holmes, Brooke. *Gender: Antiquity and Its Legacy*. New York: I. B. Taurus, 2012.

Hord, Levi C. R. "Specificity without Identity: Articulating Post-Gender Sexuality through the 'Non-binary Lesbian.'" *Sexualities* 25, no. 5–6 (2022): 615–37. https://doi.org/10.1177/1363460720981564. Published ahead of print, December 25, 2020.

Kukla, Elliot. "Terms for Gender Diversity in Classical Jewish Texts." *TransTorah*, 2006. http://www.transtorah.org/PDFs/Classical_Jewish_Terms_for_Gender_Diversity.pdf.

Mecca, Tommi Avicolli. "Brushes with Lily Law." In *The Stonewall Reader*, edited by the New York Public Library, 251–57. New York: Penguin Books, 2019.

Seidman, Naomi. *Faithful Renderings: Jewish–Christian Difference and the Politics of Translation*. Chicago: University of Chicago Press, 2006.

Strassfeld, Max K. *Trans Talmud: Androgynes and Eunuchs in Rabbinic Literature*. Oakland: University of California Press, 2022.

Contributors

Dr. Marla Brettschneider is an award-winning author and professor of political theory with a joint appointment in women's and gender studies and political science at the University of New Hampshire, where she has chaired both of her departments and founded queer studies, social justice leadership studies, and a graduate program in feminist studies. She has published numerous works in Jewish queer and diversity studies, including (from SUNY Press) *The Family Flamboyant: Race Politics, Queer Families, Jewish Lives* and *Jewish Feminism and Intersectionality*.

Vinny Calvo Prell is a Chamoru Jew who grew up in an interfaith interracial family in Los Angeles and currently lives in Washington, DC. Calvo Prell has worked for decades doing anti-oppression work, including serving as the executive director of NUJLS, the National Union of Jewish LGBTQQI Students. She also works as a social justice educator looking at relationships between racism, xenophobia, poverty, and Jewish values at a local Jewish day school. He has bachelor of arts degrees in literature and the study of race and racism as well as a master of arts in minority and urban education.

Carol Conaway, PhD, is an associate professor emerita of women's studies at the University of New Hampshire in Durham, NH. Her interests include media studies pertaining to gender, race, class, and sexual orientation; nineteenth-century African American women feminists; African and African American Jewry; and Jewish feminism. She is writing a memoir of her life as an African American lesbian who is a Jew by choice. The author of various articles, she is coeditor of the award-winning *Black Women's Intellectual Traditions: Speaking their Minds* (2007).

Lauren Hakimi is a writer and journalist in New York. Her work has been published in *CNN*, *WNYC/Gothamist*, *Bon Appétit*, *BuzzFeed News*, *The Forward*, *Jewish Telegraphic Agency*, *New York Jewish Week*, *J. The Jewish News of Northern California*, *Hey Alma*, *Lilith* magazine, and more. In spring 2022, she graduated from CUNY Hunter College with degrees in history and English literature.

A. S. Hakkâri is a child of Kurdish refugees who fled to the US following the Al-Anfal campaign. Raised balanced between two worlds—the ancient spirituality of a nostalgic homeland and the rationalist modernity of (US) America—and having reclaimed her family's hidden Jewish identity, she has been enamored with studying the politics, history, myths, and religious development of her homeland.

Joy Ladin, former David and Ruth Gottesman Chair in English at Yeshiva University, is an out transwoman and has published nine books of poetry and two books of creative nonfiction, *Through the Door of Life: A Jewish Journey between Genders* and *The Soul of the Stranger: Reading God and Torah from a Transgender Perspective*. She serves on the board of Keshet, an organization devoted to full inclusion of LGTBQ Jews in the Jewish world; links to her poems and essays are available at wordpress.joyladin.com.

Rabbi and Dr. **Sarra Lev** is a lesbian scholar who teaches Talmud and Midrash at the Reconstructionist Rabbinical College in Philadelphia. The events in her life that have had the most influence on her thinking have been her participation in socialist youth movements, walking across the United States on the Great Peace March, and living in the Women's Encampment for a Future of Peace and Justice. She is the author of two books queering Talmud.

Rona Matlow, MAJEd, MAJS, MEM, is a retired US Navy nuclear engineering officer and rabbi. Ze works as a community activist and educator in Las Vegas, Nevada. Ze came out as transgender in 2015 and nonbinary in 2019. Ze has written extensively on the topic of gender identity and how it relates to Jewish law.

Ruben Shimonov is an educator, community builder, and social entrepreneur passionate about Jewish diversity and intercultural understanding. He previously served as the director of community engagement and education at Queens College Hillel. Currently, he is the national director of Sephardi House and young leadership at the American Sephardi Federation. He is also the founding executive director of the Sephardic Mizrahi Q Network as well as director of educational experiences and programming for the Muslim-Jewish Solidarity Committee. As a visual artist, he uses his multilingual Arabic-Hebrew-Persian calligraphy to build Muslim-Jewish interfaith bridges. He has been listed among the *Jewish Week*'s "36 under 36" emerging leaders and changemakers. He is an alumnus of the Nahum Goldmann Fellowship and the Schusterman Foundation's ROI Summit for his work in Jewish social innovation and education. He has lectured extensively on the histories and cultures of Sephardic and Mizrahi communities.

Sabrina Sojourner works at the intersection of Jewish, feminist, queer, and Jew of Color spirituality and community building. She is a Jewish spiritual leader and community chaplain and a life-cycle officiant, educator, and writer. She is a member of the Association of Professional Chaplains, the National Association of Jewish Chaplains, the National Women's Studies Association, and the Women Cantors' Network.

Dr. Leonard Stein is a literary scholar, musician, and writer. He received his PhD from the University of Toronto Centre for Comparative Literature and Anne Tanenbaum Centre for Jewish Studies. He researches Sephardic literature, early modern English literature, crypto-Jewish identity, and the intersections between music and literature. He also composes music to medieval Jewish poetry.

Marielle Tawil (she/her), LMSW, is a recent graduate of Columbia School of Social Work and an active community member of the Sephardic Mizrahi Q Network. She is a psychotherapist and is passionate about serving and working with the LGBTQ+ community. She received her BA in English literature from New York University, where she also minored in child and adolescent mental health studies and Hebrew and Judaic studies.

Anonymous is of Balkan and Jewish descent and was raised in an interfaith family.

Index